REFLECTING AT KNOCK

Thomas J

Reflecting at Knock

the columba press

Thomas Lane CM

Reflecting at Knock

BEFORE OUR MERCIFUL LAMB

the columba press

First published in 2007 by
the columba press
55A Spruce Avenue, Stillorgan Industrial Park,
Blackrock, Co Dublin

Cover by Bill Bolger
based on a photograph by Philip Stratford
Origination by The Columba Press
Printed in Ireland by ColourBooks Ltd, Dublin

ISBN 978 1 85607 581 7

Acknowledgements
In my reflections on the marriage-feast of the Lamb, I have been helped
by *The Lamb's Supper*, by Scott Hahn (Doubleday, 1999). In trying to
capture the unchanging spirit of Knock, I have been inspired by
Providence my Guide, by Dame Judy Coyne (Mercier, 2004). The first reflection is a revised version of Chapter 23 of my *The Cry of Christians*
(The Columba Press, 2000). The ninth reflection is based on my article
'Finding Mary at Home' (*Doctrine and Life*, June 2004) The biblical text
used is the New Revised Standard Version, copyright © 1989, by the di-
vision of Christian Education of the National Council of Churches of
Christ in the United States of America. Used by permission.

Table of Contents

Introduction   7

Reflection One   *Introducing the Lamb*   9

Reflection Two   *A Shrine of Mercy*   22

Reflection Three   *Life's Contradictions and Tensions*   35

Reflection Four   *The Lamb is our Lamp*   46

Reflection Five   *Washed White in the Lamb's Blood*   57

Reflection Six   *Jesus both Lamb and Lion*   70

Reflection Seven   *Bringing the Multitudes*
                                    before the Lamb   80

Reflection Eight   *The Lamb will Conquer*   92

Reflection Nine   *Where Mary is at Home*   104

Reflection Ten   *An atmosphere and a place*   115

Introduction

Since the beginning of the new millennium, I have been a chaplain at Knock shrine. Day by day, I have been growing in my conviction that the apparition of 1879 is a powerful expression of the central mystery of our faith. As I move in prayer from figure to figure, I find myself getting in touch with every item of the Creed that is dear to the church. Early in 2006, I gladly accepted an invitation to provide five days of reflection for a summer school at Seton Hall College, New Jersey. I was told that I could choose my own topic. I decided to share the good news of the Lamb of God that had meant so much to me over the previous six years.

With some important modifications and several additions, I have re-arranged my Seton Hall material as a series of extended reflections for anybody who might wish to spend a day or several days of meditative prayer at the shrine of the Lamb, or some time at home in the spirit of the shrine. The reflections are presented in a way that encourages continual pauses for a prayerful lifting up of the heart. My hope is that what I have written will help some of the countless people who pray on the message of Knock to bring the good news of the triumph of the Lamb wherever they go.

My thanks to Mgr Joseph Quinn and Fr Richard Gibbons who read the text and made valuable suggestions. Margaret Doyle has, with her usual patience, prepared the whole text. I thank her, along with Jane Foley who gave me much practical help at Knock.

Thomas Lane CM
Paschal time 2007

Reflection One

Introducing the Lamb

The day I received my first Holy Communion, my mother gave me a very precious gift. She handed me a small silver locket and she asked me to treasure it all my life. She explained to me that the locket was called an *Agnus Dei* and that the words meant Lamb of God. On one side of the locket was the figure of the cross of Christ. On the other side was the image of a lamb. Later I was to learn that the locket contained wax from a Paschal candle and the relic of a saint, presumably a martyr.

My first communion day was a very good introduction to the Lamb of God. Over the years I have heard of many beautiful representations of the mystery of the Lamb. There is none more thought-provoking and prayer-provoking than the one at the gable wall at Knock.

Hard times
The original apparition took place during hard times. They were the times of a second famine in Ireland. My mother was born about seven years later. From the accounts she gave me of her childhood, I can only conclude that, along with her neighbours, she had her share of hard times. Having completed her primary school education, she was one of thousands who emi-

grated from Cobh to Boston to earn a modest fortune. The years that surrounded my first introduction to the Lamb of God were the hard times in which people endured the grimness of annuities and an economic war in the years leading up to the Second World War. All of this would seem to indicate that the Lamb of God is particularly close to people at any times that can be called hard. Indeed our principal introduction to the sacrificial lamb in the Bible is in the descriptions of the annual ritual of the slaying of a lamb. This was part of the celebrations of a people going out of a land of bondage (cf Exodus 12).

The Lamb of God who takes away our sins by his blood continues to have a strong prominence in our celebrations of who we are as Christians. The church has come to see the Lamb as identical with the Suffering Servant of God who was crushed with pain for the sins of the many and was like a lamb led to the slaughter (Isa 53). It is significant that we give prominence to the Lamb not just in some Masses but in every Mass. Every time we proclaim the mystery of faith, we celebrate the genius of God who brings life where there seemed to be only death. Drawing on such sources as the Book of Revelation, the Easter church gives almost daily expression to the paradoxes of a divine plan in which the Lamb gathers the sheep and God keeps turning the tables on those who thought that subtle human schemes are better than God's wisdom.

Hard times again

The Lamb once slain continues to be the supporter of all those who are going through hard times. Nobody would claim that we live in the kind of hard times that prevailed in 1879 and intermittently through to the Second World War and after. We are living not in a time of economic war but in a time of an economic boom that would have been unimaginable even in the not too distant past. But it is a hard time to be fully Christian and to follow the Lamb 'wherever he goes' (Rev 14:4), not just along the ways that are humanly attractive. In Europe generally, Christians have been experiencing many forms of decline. Quite a few of our spiritual wells have been running dry. In Ireland, the decline has sometimes been steep. There are times when we cannot help recalling the Lord's question: 'When the Son of Man comes, will he find faith on earth?' (Luke 18:8).

In this situation, one could speculate as to whether our society today is more or less sinful than what prevailed in the economically hard times of the past. It is a largely futile question. A sinless society has never existed. The work of the slaughtered Lamb somehow reaches back to the foundation of the world (Rev 13:8). What is certain is that the sins of our society, religious and secular, past and present, are coming into the open today in a way that they did not get a chance to do in the past. We are experiencing a striking expression of the Lord's words that nothing is hidden that will not be disclosed (Luke 8:17).

One is reminded of the work of the good housewife who boils the local berries and removes the scum that comes to the surface before she gives us something that delights our taste. In the various boilings over of present day anger about the secret sins and hypocrisies of our society, much scum has been coming to the top. This is good for us. But we often find ourselves uncertain as to what to do with the scum. We know that we must at the same time reject it and love our fellow-sinner in whom it surfaces. We feel a new urge to cry out to the Lamb of God who alone can take away our sins, who alone can bring us God's mercy, who alone can give us peace.

The help of two evangelists
In interpreting the message of the silent figures in the Knock apparition, figures that are now represented in marble in the chapel of the apparition, we are particularly helped by two evangelists. The first of these is John.

- John the evangelist, who in many ways tends to be identified with the apostle John, was himself one of the figures in the apparition;

- He is holding the book of the gospel in his hand and he is clothed as a bishop;

- The key to what he is telling us must surely be the first chapter of his gospel;

- He tells us about the Word that was in the beginning (1:1);

- about another John who was sent by God (1:6) and to whom the original Knock parish church was dedicated;
- about the Word becoming flesh and living among us (1:14), and about John the baptiser recognising him as the Lamb who takes sin away (1:29);
- about the call of some of the first apostles, about Nathaniel who was told that he would see heaven opened and the angels of God ascending and descending upon the Son of Man (1:51);

• The episcopal clothing is a clear indicator that it is the call of those who continue the mission of the apostles of the Lamb (cf Rev 21:14) to teach the whole mystery of the Word made flesh and to be witnesses of the same Word. For John, the Word made flesh is identical with the innocent Lamb who alone can undo the damage done by our lack of innocence.

The gospel according to St John contains no infancy narrative; neither does it contain an explicit invitation to become as little children. One could say that the equivalent of these is the identification of the Word made flesh with the sinless but sin-bearing Lamb. We have close connections here with the images of the Lamb in the Book of Revelation and the special Easter Sequence. We are given a key to the Christian under-standing:
- of what it is to be a willing victim;
- of the sacrifice that comes straight from the heart;

- of God making Christ to be sin so that we may become righteous (2 Cor 5:21);
- of the just one dying for the unjust (1 Pet 3:18).

Light from St Matthew
Though he was not himself a figure in the apparition,
the second evangelist who can help us to interpret the
Knock event is Matthew.

- St Matthew is the only evangelist who tells us
  about the flight of the Holy Family into Egypt and
  about their return from there;

- All the Knock figures are standing;

- One cannot help thinking that they are expressing
  their readiness to go, to enter into hard times in the
  alien land associated with the ancient bondage of
  the house of Israel as described in Genesis and
  Exodus;

- Their reason for going was that Herod was searching for the child to destroy him (Mt 2:13ff);

- This search was followed by the massacre of the in-
  nocents;

- The stay in Egypt was to last until those who were
  seeking the child's life were dead;

As we re-read this story of the Holy Family's flight
into Egypt and of their exodus from there, we cannot
miss the resonances with the original story of the
going down into Egypt and of the exodus that was to
be annually celebrated by the festive sacrifice of a

lamb. It is easy too to see the word of hope for a people who were experiencing hard times when the gable wall at Knock was lit up by the apparition of the Lamb:

- There is an unmistakable message here for the church and for the whole human family in new forms of exile, exodus and desert that we have been recently experiencing;

- Words like massacre and abuse make frequent appearances in our daily news;

- The prophets of our day alert us to ways we are to find the presence of God in new testings, new deserts;

- People like Dom Helder Camara have told us that preaching justice and peace in today's society calls for a new willingness to live in the desert and to listen to what the voice of God is saying to us there.

Knock: a continual call to family
The Holy Family at the gable wall at Knock have a message for the whole human family in whatever bondage or freeing from bondage we are now experiencing:

- They help us to come to the Father who alone knows the Son and to the Son who alone knows the Father and reveals him to anybody he chooses (Mt 11:27);

- The Father to whom the Holy Family leads us is

the Father from whom all fatherhood, all motherhood, all sisterhood, all brotherhood in heaven and
on earth takes its name (cf Eph 3:15);

• Each time we look at the family we call holy we are
  encouraged to wish and to pray that something of
  both the sinlessness and the courage that held
  them together will pervade our families and
  church communities for the building up of which
  St Matthew, in his gospel, gives us so many detailed prescriptions.

St Matthew has something very special to tell us
about each of the persons:
- to whom so many devout people 'give their hearts
  and their souls';
- from whom so many devout people seek 'assist-
  ance in their last agony';
- in the peace of whom so many devout people hope
  to 'breathe forth their souls'.

• He encourages us to look at Joseph, the 'righteous
  man' (Mt 1:19) who was given the impossible task
  of getting up, taking the child and his mother and
  fleeing into Egypt for an indefinite period of time
  (2:13);

• He encourages us to discover again the very valid
  reasons why the church has, in various times, given
  Joseph the titles of protector, guardian, custodian;

• He helps us to appreciate the validity of the in-
  stincts of St Teresa of Avila who, when she set out
  on journeys outside her own community, placed

the statue of St Joseph on her chair and asked him to look after the house in her absence as he did when she was present.

St Matthew invites us to look at the woman who is the mother of the child with whom we must identify if we wish to enter the kingdom of heaven (18: 3).

- This is the child who is Emmanuel, God with us (Mt 1: 23);

- This is the child whom the pilgrim Magi saw after they followed the star;

- This is the child who filled them with joy as they found him with Mary his mother, knelt down, paid homage and offered gifts (2:7-11).

As we look at Mary in the Knock perspective, we cannot help recognising her as the mother of all pilgrims, ready to be part of our sorrowful mysteries as well as of our joyful and glorious ones, and of our mysteries of light. This mother of pilgrims is identical with the woman whom the evangelist John portrays as the mother of disciples (cf 19:26, 27).

The child at the centre
The Jesus of the Knock apparition is the Jesus who is at the centre of the Holy Family and who alerts us to whatever destroys the child in ourselves and in others.

- He wishes to be at the centre of every family along all of life's journey, all our entries into any land of bondage and our exits out of it;

- For Matthew, he is the child;

- For John the baptiser and John the evangelist, he is the Lamb of God taking away the sin of the world;

- As we contemplate him on the first page of the gospel which John the apostle-evangelist is holding in his hand, the gospel which is the life-programme for all those who continue the mission of the original apostles and evangelists, we recognise him as the one who was in the beginning with God and who was himself God;

- We recognise him as the Word who became flesh and set up his dwelling place among us;

- We recognise him as the one who still wishes to set up his dwelling place wherever people are.

As Christians, we can never see our earthly dwelling place as a 'lasting city' (Heb 13:14). It is more in the nature of a temporary lodging place. The playwright Jerome K. Jerome wrote a beautiful work called *The Passing of the Third Floor Back*. It is the story of a disgruntled group who find themselves together in a lodging house. Their relationships with each other are very far from what one would wish to find in an ideal human group. They are, in fact, characterised by hatred and mutual criticism. Into the motley company comes an unknown stranger who is more than content to occupy the least attractive room in the house. His loving and unselfish presence soon transforms the group and makes them recognise each other as brothers and sisters building each other up in mutual concern and love. The Christian interpretation of the play is plain for all to see. Here indeed is a glimpse of the Word who has become flesh and who, under many guises, keeps dwelling among us, in our journey to the only dwelling place that will last.

Agents of the Lamb

All believers in Jesus Christ are called to be agents of the Lamb who keeps taking away the sins of the world.

- Each of us is called to co-operate with the Word in his becoming enfleshed and accompanying people into and out of the many forms of human bondage;

- Each of us does this in the perspectives of a particular tradition, in particular hard times, at a particular now;

- It has been said that the experience of hard times can lead any of us to do one of four things. We could decide to ignore, or to deplore, or to restore, or to explore.
  - The ignorer decides not to face the reality;
  - The deplorer laments the passing of better times;
  - The restorer sets out to bring back the way things were in the better times;
  - The explorer asks what can be done now and how it can best be done.

As agents of the Lamb, we are not called to ignore or to deplore. We are called to keep exploring and to pray for the wisdom as to how we can help to restore

God's plan by 'gathering up all things in Christ' (cf Eph 1:10). With Christ, we are all makers of a new world.

Angels ascending and descending
The witnesses of the apparition at Knock saw angels hovering about the Lamb.

- As I pray in the shrine at the gable wall, I come to realise that the angels of God are still 'ascending and descending to where the Son of Man is' (Jn 1:51) and that the risen Son of Man is close to both our right hand and the Father's right hand.

- I come to realise that the angels are God's messengers, ever active in our two-way communication with God, earth to heaven and heaven to earth.

- In the intimacy of this communication, I come to realise that there is still light on the whole church's gable wall and that this light continues to be the 'light of all people' (Jn 1:4).

- I come to realise that the 'marriage of the Lamb' (Rev 19:7) has not been called off.

- I am encouraged to keep washing myself white in his blood (cf Rev 7:14).

- I am reminded that I am an agent of the beautiful plan of an all-wise God who keeps bringing triumph where there seemed to be nothing but failure.

The cross
The cross of the Lamb was prominent in the Knock apparition.

- The cross and Lamb continue to throw light on each other;

- The figure of the Lamb standing on the eucharistic altar of sacrifice, under the shadow of the cross, assures me that, in spite of all the glooms that might encircle us, the sin of the world is continually being taken away;

- It makes me thank God for reassuring an oppressed people in their belief that it is the Mass that matters;

- The piece of wax between cross and Lamb in my first communion gift is a continual assurance to me that the Paschal candle is always giving light, at Easter time and outside it;

- The relic of the martyr is an assurance to me that the various forms of the cross of martyrdom are not in vain;

- It helps me to interpret the message of Oscar Romero and of the lifeblood of the many other martyrs of our own time;

- It invites me to look up at the victorious cloud of witnesses that intercede for us as we try to persevere in running life's race (cf Heb 12:1);

The unchanging good news is that the Lamb, though slain, is alive and calling us all to be fully alive.

Reflection Two

A Shrine of Mercy

I like to call it the shrine of the Lamb of God;
- Sometimes I call it the shrine of the Eucharist;
- It is most commonly described as a shrine of Mary.

There is no conflict between these approaches. In common with many other descriptions of the shrine, each of them alerts us to the nearness of God's holiness and of God's mercy.

• Each of them invites us to enter more deeply into the riches of the communion of saints, that great network of all holy persons and holy things, in heaven, on earth and in purgatory;

• Each of them invites us to throw ourselves into the arms of the God of mercy who saved us by the sacrifice of the Lamb of mercy.

In the *Gloria* of the Mass, we address Jesus Christ as the Lamb of God who takes away the sins of the world; we go on to say that, along with the Father and the Holy Spirit, Jesus Christ alone is holy.

• We ask this holy Lamb of God to have mercy on us;

• Later in the Mass, we ask him, twice again, to have mercy on us;

22

- We ask that, in the same mercy, he will give us his peace;

- When his eucharistic body is held up before us, we are assured that we are indeed looking at the Lamb of God who takes sins away and that we are blessed to be among those called to his supper.

Our merciful God
We are used to saying that the God who 'again and again offered us a covenant' (cf Eucharistic Prayer IV) has two great qualities: mercy and faithfulness. In fact, the two are one: unfailing mercy. This mercy is God's compassionate love which keeps taking us by surprise when we feel completely unworthy of it.

Each of the saints gives us a new perspective on God's mercy. People like St Vincent de Paul were continually experiencing its depths.

- St Vincent's whole life became a song of thanks to the God whose unfailing mercy kept touching his own life and calling him to be its carrier to others;

- He became inebriated with this unfailing mercy;

- He kept detecting the need of it in the people whom the gospel describes as the least, the lost, the last;

- As a result, he kept motivating others to be agents of the same mercy;

- With St Louise de Marillac and many women and men collaborators, he taught them how to bring it to those in the direst forms of poverty and in the countless forms of alienation that are recognised by those who see with the eyes of the God of compassionate love, of unfailing mercy.

To help all of us keep our eyes fixed on our merciful God, Pope John Paul II gave the new name of 'Divine Mercy Sunday' to the Sunday after Easter Sunday. He wasn't diverting our attention from the riches of the Easter mystery. He was inviting us to see the passion, death and resurrection of Jesus as the limitless outpouring of the Father's mercy.

Mother of Mercy
At the Knock shrine, we are introduced to the merciful Lamb of God by the woman we address as both merciful and holy. We address her as both 'Mother of Mercy' and 'Holy Mother of God'.

- Mary is mother of the merciful Lamb of God and of the countless people who benefit from and are agents of God's mercy.

- In Knock she is looking up to heaven from where all mercy comes.

- In the first accounts of the apparition, she herself seemed to occupy the most prominent place. When we put all the accounts together, it becomes clear that what is distinctive about this Marian shrine is the presence of the Lamb of God. Mary is drawing our attention to him as he keeps having mercy on us and giving us his peace.

- She is doing this in the atmosphere of holiness that is the communion of saints.

- With her are two of the most significant members of that communion, St Joseph and St John.

- Each of these great saints reminds us that we are a redeemed people. As I read the best of recent writing on Mary and reflect on new ecumenical approaches to her, I am helped to see clearly who is my only redeemer and who makes me part of a redeemed people.

At the very same time, I keep thanking our one redeemer for involving all of us in his saving work of mercy, along with Mary who, precisely because she is mother of the redeemer, is mother of mercy. There is no competition between the redeeming Christ and any of the rest of the communion of saints.

Knock: a beacon of God's unfailing mercy
Each generation has had its own perspectives on the way Jesus involves all of us his disciples in helping each other on our journey to heaven. Each in its own way came to recognise the special place of Mary, in her unique relationship with Father, Son and Spirit. I am sure that those who experienced the apparition in 1879 had no sophisticated understanding of the ties between the Lamb of God, his mother, St Joseph and St John in the merciful work of our redemption. In the beginning, they didn't all recognise all the figures. Mary Byrne helped them by what she had seen during her holiday in Lecanvey. In the original accounts

of what they saw, the witnesses varied somewhat in details. Indeed the background story and the collective witness of all the privileged fifteen bear the marks and limitations of human beings describing an apparition from the invisible world of the God whom nobody has ever seen (cf Jn 1:18).

I am sometimes asked do I really believe in Knock. My answer is that I believe in the reality expressed in all the items of the Creed, beginning with Father, Son and Holy Spirit and ending with the communion of saints, the forgiveness of sins, the resurrection of the body and life everlasting. I go on to say that I regard Knock as a wonderful coming alive of all these truths of faith;
- that, like the commissions in 1879 and 1936, I trust the witnesses in their evidence;
- that the fruits of their experience have been remarkably wholesome;
- that I continue to be impressed by these fruits;
- that no attempts to explain away what happened on that evening in 1879 have been convincing.

When I try to understand the interacting between heaven and earth on the evening of the apparition and what led up to it, I realise that when a group of very ordinary people are invited into such a special communication with heaven, one cannot draw easy lines between God's part and the human part. The Lord and his mother speak to us in the language and images of wherever we are housed now and wherever we are coming from now. Knock is a lovely example of a homely meeting of heaven and earth. It is God's unfailing mercy in action.

When we see the end-product of the apparition as represented by the designing and arranging of the figures that now enhance the space beside the gable wall, we cannot but marvel.

- They are the result of much remembering, much consultation, much loving workmanship, much generosity.

- They highlight the action that is central to the eucharistic sacrifice.

- The merciful Lamb of God is standing victorious on the altar.

- Above the altar is a representation of the cross from which he was taken down.

- The angels of God are linking heaven and earth, ascending and descending around where the Lamb is (cf Jn 1:51).

- Where the merciful Lamb is, there the saints are. Three key figures from the communion of saints are inviting us to share in the victory of the merciful Lamb.

- For Christians, all this message is timeless. Each generation, each new pilgrim, can bring out of its treasure what is new and what is old (cf Mt 13: 52).

The Passover sacrifice of the merciful Lamb

For years, I was somewhat uneasy about the fact that the detailed, dare I say gory, description of the Passover Lamb should have such a prominent place in the Mass of Holy Thursday. I didn't think it blended gracefully with the accounts of the gentle washing of the disciples' feet and of the supper that followed. But, as I became absorbed in the message of Knock, I learned to approach Holy Week and Easter as the extended feast of the Merciful Lamb.

The setting for Holy Week is presented with varying details in all the four gospels.

• On Palm Sunday, we read that on the first day of unleavened bread, when the Passover Lamb was sacrificed, the disciples asked Jesus where did he want them to go and make preparations for the Passover (Mk 14:12ff). The Passover, the Pasch, was the annual celebration of God's chosen people coming out of Egypt. A lamb was sacrificed. His blood was smeared on the doorposts of the houses. God was asked to save his chosen people and to 'pass over' the houses of those being freed from slavery.

• On Holy Thursday, we celebrate the meal that was the result of the Passover celebrations. As Jesus sat down with his disciples, it began to emerge that he himself was the Lamb of sacrifice, freely offering himself and giving himself as true food and true drink to his disciples (cf Jn 6:55). All the details from the Passover chapter in Exodus (12:1ff) began to come to life.

- The spirit of the Passover is continued through Good Friday when the Lamb was led to the slaughter, never opening his mouth (Isa 53:7).

- On both Holy Thursday and Good Friday, we are a remembering people, brought into existence by a remembering God. We thank God for the forgiveness that comes as the sacrificial body is given and the blood is poured out.

- By the time we come to celebrate the Vigil Mass on Holy Saturday night, we joyfully say 'he is the true Lamb who took away the sin of the world'.

The Easter victory of the merciful Lamb
For the whole of the Easter season, we joyfully celebrate the victory of the sacrificed Lamb.

- At Morning Prayer on Easter Sunday, we thank God for 'the spotless Lamb who, more than due, paid for his sheep'.

- At Easter Sunday Mass, we have a special Sequence praising the Lamb who has redeemed the sheep.

- The first Easter preface puts it all in perspective: '… when Christ became our Paschal sacrifice. He is the true Lamb who took away the sins of the world; by dying he destroyed our death; by rising he restored our life'.

- All five Easter prefaces remind us that Christ became our Paschal sacrifice. The third of the five describes Christ as 'the victim who dies no more, the Lamb once slain who lives forever'.

- The good news of the Lamb pervades all our praying and singing during the whole of the Easter season.

- The most characteristic Easter hymn begins with 'At the Lamb's high feast we sing'. It focuses our attention on 'love the victim, love the priest'. Christ the Lamb is praised as 'Paschal victim, Paschal bread'.

- An antiphon on Thursday of Easter Week describes the new Easter believers as 'new-born lambs crying out *alleluia* as they stand before the Lamb clothed in white garments'.

There are suggestions of spring freshness in all the *alleluia* season. Many people today say that we are in a winter time in the church. More than once before his death, Pope John Paul II expressed his conviction that we are on the verge of a new springtime. A similar note was struck by Pope Benedict XVI when he called for a synod on the word of God. If we really are an *alleluia* people and believe in Jesus Christ as our Paschal Lamb, we have no option but to identify with this expression of Christian optimism. On many levels, the Easter Lamb suggests springtime. This sense of spring helps us to cope with our many winters. Mark Twain once said that many a day in New England can bring all four seasons. Not a bad description of many a day in the life of the church!

The book of the Merciful Lamb

The liturgy of the Easter season is a good introduction to the Apocalypse, the Book of Revelation. I have come to call it 'The Book of the Merciful Lamb'. It can be a bewildering book and many a reader has put it down in frustration.

- After some instructions and words of encouragement to several local churches, all of whom had been experiencing trials and testings, it describes a world inhabited by a wide range of good as well as not so good people, and a whole range of attractive and not so attractive animals.

- They are all interacting with each other and with good angels and not so good angels on the whole stage of earth, sky and sea. On this great stage, there are many struggles, many battles. In each of the great struggles, Jesus the Lamb of God is somehow involved. He is dealing with enemies who come in many shapes, sizes and colours.

- In the accounts of the struggles, we are introduced to various groups of seven, some of them friendly, some of them hostile. There are many dark symbols. We read of a dark, bottomless pit, of scrolls that cannot be opened, of woes and destructive plagues (ch 9), of bowls of God's wrath (ch 16), of a lake of fire and sulphur (ch 20:10).

In recent years, I have been reading the book as a description of the many states and activities of the Merciful Lamb of God, in his continual saving activity in every struggle in every part of our universe. It all leads up to his saving victory which has implications for everybody and everything in the whole of creation.

- In the book of the Merciful Lamb, he is at some stages presented as a helpless, sacrificial victim (5: 12); at other times, he is presented as radiant in glory (21: 11). From the experience of both states, he emerges as King of kings and Lord of lords (19: 16). His robe dipped in blood is the garment of final victory (v 13).

- In that victory, he leads the liturgy in the glory of what we simply call heaven. The Book of the Merciful Lamb calls it by such names as the New Jerusalem, the holy city of God, the marriage feast of the Lamb, a new heaven and a new earth, the home of God (21: 1-3).

- This final victory unites all the well-nigh countless allusions to the Lamb.

- Even the beasts declare his victory and fall down before him (ch 5).

- He alone can open what has been sealed (6: 1).

- He can nourish and lead in the way of the Good Shepherd (7: 17).

- His relationship with the redeemed is described in the joyful imagery of the marriage-feast (chs 19 and 21).

- Those who follow him are called the chosen, the faithful (17:14).

- The new Jerusalem, which will be the final dwelling place of all of us who keep following the Lamb, will have the glory of God as its light and the Lamb himself as its lamp (21:23). No wonder we call ourselves a people of hope! The Book of the Merciful Lamb is indeed a book of hope.

Mercy touching all creation

As I read the Book of the Merciful Lamb, I can't help wondering whether writers like C. S. Lewis, notably in his Narnia books, were influenced by the benign and not so benign animals in the vision that the 'seer' John experienced in Patmos (cf Rev 1:9). Recent studies of human origins draw our attention to our many affinities with the rest of the animal world. Into the mouths of talking animals, Lewis, sensitive to these affinities, put many words of wisdom about human behaviour.

Before ever there was a whisper about the possibility of evolution, Pope St Gregory the Great wondered why Jesus told the eleven to proclaim the good news not to all people but to the whole of creation (Mk 16:15). His answer was that the whole of creation is in the human being. We have, he said, being in common with stones, life in common with plants, feeling in common with other animals, and intelligence in common with angels. The Book of the Lamb and the Narnia stories explore some of the implications of our close association with animals, all animals, and that our leader is, at the same time, Lamb and Lion.

Both St Gregory and C. S. Lewis remind us that every one of us carries around the whole of creation in a fragile, mortal body. But we are not alone as we carry such a treasure in clay jars (cf 2 Cor 4:7).

- We are at all times immersed in the communion of all holy persons and all holy things.

- We are in the palm of the hand of the Father of all mercies and supported by the countless agents of the Father's mercy.

- The Merciful Lamb continues to take away our sins.

- Though he alone is holy, he invites us to share in his holiness.

- He sends each of us a personal invitation to share in his great banquet. This is the final flowering of all his acts of mercy

- At every Eucharist we get a taste of what the great final banquet will be like. We await that banquet in joyful hope.

Reflection Three

Life's Contradictions and Tensions

The Book of Revelation has apparently contradictory things to say about the Lamb of God:

- Though gentle, he is wrathful (6:16);

- He washes us white in his red blood (7:14);

- He is slaughtered and yet he is victorious (5:9ff).

We are introduced here to what the English Catholic writer, G. K. Chesterton, called the paradoxes of Christianity. In a paradox, statements that seem to be contradictories are shown to be equally true. A chapter in one of Chesterton's best known books describes how, in his journey into the Catholic Church, he found Catholics being the object of what seemed to be totally contradictory charges.

- They were, for example, accused of being too timid and too warlike;

- being wearers of sackcloth and of pompous garments;

- being only for some chosen people and being for all people.

As he reflected on the countless contradictions and apparent contradictions, Chesterton came to realise the church's unique ability to live with, and even draw life from opposites. The church, he said, is not a lover of pink; her preferred colours are red and white.

Chesterton's insights into the paradoxes of Christianity help us to live with the many contradictions and apparent contradictions in our day to day living, and in the demands of the gospel to lose our life in order to save it (Mk 8:35) and to be last in order to be first (Lk 13:30). Even in the course of one day, there can be many experiences that just don't add up. We can find ourselves asking 'Did I really do that?'

- We learn to have sympathy with St Paul as he experienced contradictions between the law of God written in his heart and the law in action in his unruly members (Rom 7);

- We learn to make sense of and identify with the gentle St Francis of Assisi who is said to have gone into a great rage when he found his brethren offending against his understanding of poverty by building a house of stone in Bologna;

- We learn to see how Jesus could describe himself as both meek and humble of heart (Mt 11:29) and as the successful burglar of the house of Satan (Lk 11:21, 22);

- We learn to understand how, in the Easter imagery, the Lamb is the one who redeemed the sheep;

- We learn to see how Jesus Christ is, at the same time, both in the glory of heaven and 'in agony until the end of time'.

Daily tastings; daily tensions

As we try to deal with the many paradoxes of the gospel, we come to realise that what we have in our life on this earth is a series of tastings and glimpses of the great banquet in the heaven for which we are destined. This gives rise to many tensions.

- There is a tension between the ideal put before us at Mass, the realities of the rest of the day, and what won't happen until the final supper of the Lamb in heaven;

- St John put it very cleary: 'We are God's children now; what we will be has not yet been revealed' (1 Jn 3:2);

- Our liturgy here on earth is a very limited sharing in the liturgy that is going on in heaven. Both are an anticipation of the 'new heaven' (Rev 21:1);

- We get some glimpses of what this new heaven will be like in the final chapters of the Book of Revelation;

- In the new heaven and the new earth, all tears will be wiped away (Rev 21:4), and the glorified Lord who sits on the throne will make all things new (v 5);

- Life has many delights, many joys, but they are all passing. They lack the quality of the eternal now. Even in our deepest joys, we have to live with some tears of exile. We have to be satisfied with tasting and glimpsing. We do 'taste and see' in every Eucharist. The daily tasting and seeing are good for us, but, as St Paul tells us, we see now only 'in a mirror, dimly' (1 Cor 13:12);

- We can identify with the poet who had a passing experience of human love and wrote:
  'I saw her once, one little while and then no more. Earth looked like heaven a little while and then no more.'

Sacrifice, meal and memorial

Some people feel that, in our understanding of the Eucharist, there is a conflict between the words sacrifice, memorial and meal. Understood in their full context, the three are, in fact, inseparable and of equal importance. They keep throwing light on each other. If I say that the Eucharist is primarily a meal, it is important that I go on to say that it's a meal of special remembering, of special sacrificial food.

- *Sacrifice* is essentially the offering of a gift to God. The deeper the sacrifice the more it touches into, heals and nourishes the countless aspects of our relationship with God. Every sacrifice we offer has implications for others.

The offering by Jesus of his whole self to the Father, for our sake, was the perfect sacrifice. He gave himself totally, to the extent of losing all his life-blood. This happened in his suffering and dying as he went back to the Father and left us the gift of the Paschal mystery. His sacrifice was the crowning of all the known sacrifices of at-one-ment and of forgiveness that God's chosen people had ever celebrated. The dispositions of Jesus, towards his Father and towards us, made him the perfect offerer and the perfect victim willing to give his whole life away. All this we celebrate and respond to at the eucharistic sacrifice.

• The Eucharist is the great act of remembering, of *memorial*;

Nourished by his word, we thankfully remember the Lord's life, passion, death and resurrection, and his assurance that he will come again in glory.

More important, the Father remembers the whole work of his Son and he remembers all the living and the dead. When God remembers at the Eucharist, he sends his Spirit and he makes present the original saving activity of his Son.

• Sacrifice and memorial are celebrated in the *meal* at which Jesus himself keeps saying 'take and eat' and 'take and drink'. What we eat and drink are nothing less than the body given and the blood poured out.

This is the great expression of God's love, the divine *agapé* of which Pope Benedict XVI has written in his encyclical letter. The Eucharist is the daily proof that God is love itself.

Our daily anticipation of the final 'marriage of the Lamb' (Rev 19:7) keeps reminding us of the Pope's teaching that human marriage is the most foundational expression of God's burning love for his people. It also reminds us that the symbol of the meal is the most favoured biblical symbol of heaven. For this reason, it is good to read and re-read the many accounts, especially in St Luke, of the meals shared by Jesus with varying classes of people. It is also good to read and re-read what the Letter to the Ephesians has to say about the marriage-union between Christ and his church (Eph 5:25-33).

• No Eucharist will ever be a perfect expression of sacrifice, memorial, meal. Many of our celebrations of the Eucharist tend to be one-dimensional, with an under-emphasis or over-emphasis on sacrifice, or memorial, or meal. This is part of the price of our being a pilgrim church, a people who have to live with many tensions, many contradictions, many limited glimpses, many tastings.

Glimpses of the Lamb's marriage-feast
We are a church of daily tastings. We are also a church of daily seeing, or rather daily glimpsing. We thank God for the many painters and other artists who help us to have glimpses of the final heavenly victory of the Lamb.

• The recent re-furbishing of the chapel of Castleknock College, Dublin, drew attention to the fact that over the altar is a painted image of the Lamb of God. It has served as a visual entry into the mystery of the Mass for generations of young students. In the same spirit, the rose window in St Peter's church, Phibsboro, has at its centre a representation of the Lamb. St Peter's is one of many churches with such prominent images of the

Merciful Lamb of God. In the Knock parish church, an image of the Lamb has a significant place in relation to altar and tabernacle. It blends well with Knock's special monstrance of the Lamb.

• My favourite sculpture of the Lamb of God is the one in Chartres Cathedral. I saw it many years ago but it is only recently that it really spoke to me. John the Baptist is tenderly holding the Lamb in his arms. Surely this represents the final flowering of all his searching, all his austere living, all his self-diminishment, all his puzzlement, all his questioning. In the embrace of the Lamb he is ready to face a death that is the last word in absurdity.

My favourite painting of the Lamb is on the panels of the great altarpiece, *The Adoration of the Mystic Lamb*, completed by Van Eyck in Ghent in 1432.

• In a breathtaking way, it captures all the riches of what the Book of Revelation has to say about the victory of the Lamb of God that provides the setting for the great final banquet;

• The Lamb, who is identical with the risen Christ, is being adored in a garden of the heavenly Jerusalem;

• He is surrounded by angels and by human beings of all ranks;

• Our eyes are drawn up to the figure of the red-robed, enthroned Christ;

• In special nearness to him are Mary, Adam and

Eve, John the Baptist, and angels who are joyful music-makers;

- This whole feast for the eyes includes a delightful display of flowers, ever fresh water, censers of praise and adoration. All these are a fine setting for the image of the virgin reading from the book and the stream of blood into the chalice from the side of the Lamb;

- In a position central for all the panels is the pervading presence of the Father and of the Holy Spirit who is always proceeding from the Father and the Son.

Painters and altarpieces can generate curiosity. *The Adoration of the Mystic Lamb* helps one to bow down in worship. Like Knock, it makes us thank God for the wonderful blend of the themes of the Merciful Lamb and the communion of saints.

- With all their beauty, even the best of paintings and images fall infinitely short of the God who 'dwells in unapproachable light' (1 Tim 6:16). At best, they give us only a glimpse. It is no wonder that, over the centuries, new movements encouraged people to reject all images, and even to destroy them. It is also no wonder that some ways of prayer attempt to be imageless.

- But, in our journey to the new heaven and the new earth, I think most of us need some images, most of the time. As we follow the Lamb, we would do well to remember the programme much loved by

Cardinal Newman: 'From shadows and images to the truth.'

A cry in our contradictions

In dealing with the daily contradictions and tensions, and in having to be satisfied with glimpses and tastings, we find ourselves giving many a cry. In the scriptures, the human cry can be a paradoxical word. The gospels tell us of different and apparently contradictory nuances in the cries of the Lord himself and the cries of people closely associated with his mission.

- His presence in the womb of his mother made Elizabeth give a loud cry of joy (Lk 1:42);

- At what could be described as a water-festival, he cried out 'Let anyone who is thirsty come to me' (Jn 7:37);

- His loud cry at the tomb of Lazarus (Jn 11:43) was, in the same breath, a cry of pain at the ravages caused by death and a cry of victory over death;

- His cry at his own death (Mk 15:34) had the same double quality. Indeed it was in his 'loud cries and tears' (Heb 5:7) that his Father heard his prayer.

In the days when Pope John XXIII opened the windows and had us praying for a new Pentecost, many of us felt 'bliss is it in this dawn to be alive'. Since those days, we have been uttering many cries. Some of these have been cries of thanksgiving, as we recognise God's Pentecostal breathing. But we have also expressed other cries as we experience not dawn but bleak darkness, not heaven but a tinge of hell. There have been cries of surprise and cries of disappointment. Somehow there is a feeling today that the whole church is in the cry and labour pains of some new birthing which we are, as yet, unable to name. We are learning that only God's Spirit can ensure a healthy and joyful birth.

Out of the depths
The *Prayer of the Church* provides us with wonderful resources for all our range of cries, in all our experience of tensions, contradictions and apparent contradictions.

- Many of the psalms take the form of a cry to the Lord. Foremost in these is the psalm *Out of the depths* (Ps 130). We are used to looking on this psalm as a prayer for the dead. In fact, it is very much a prayer of the living;

- The psalmist cries out of the depths of the human heart;

- The psalm is a cry of hope, from the human depths into the depths of God;

- The cry is to the God of steadfast love, the God who has great power to redeem;

- The cry is of one waiting for the Lord and hoping in his word;

- It is the cry of one waiting more than those who watch for the morning.

The cry of *Out of the depths* is captured in many other psalms, notably in the ones about the soul thirsting for God, like the deer longing for flowing streams (Ps 42) and about the soul clinging to God (Ps 63).

- All these psalms are the cries of people who experienced contradictions;

- All of them are shot through with the great virtue of hope which keeps us anchored to God (cf Heb 6:19).

For Christians, the cry that sums up all cries is the one to God as 'Abba, Father'. This was the cry of Jesus in the agony which had the makings of his final ecstasy (Mk 14:36). The Spirit who raised the agonising and dying Jesus from the dead enables us to cry 'Abba, Father' (Rom 8:15) and to rejoice that we are heirs to a whole new heaven and a whole new earth. In that new creation, we will be beyond tasting and glimpsing; we will see God 'as he is' (1 Jn 3:2); we will see him 'face to face' (1 Cor 13:12). Could we ever hope for more?

Reflection Four

The Lamb is our Lamp (Rev 21:23)

The first lamp I ever saw was in our living room at home. It was a paraffin oil lamp. In the dark winter evenings, it lit up the whole kitchen and, in a sense, the whole house. It was the only light we had for doing our school exercises and for my father as he reached up for a read of the old 'Fifth Book'. It could be quite temperamental. Sometimes the wick would get a bit contrary and it had to be coaxed to come right with the help of a scissors and my mother's deft fingers. On a ledge in front of the Sacred Heart picture was a tiny lamp that kept lighting, day and night, providing another kind of light. Beside lamp and picture was the Act of Consecration to the Sacred Heart, with the signature of everybody in the house. All this was the fruit of a great movement of evangelisation in Ireland around the time of the Eucharistic Congress in 1932.

- In each of the bedrooms of the house was a candle to keep us from complete darkness at times of our rising and going to bed.

- Some of our neighbours had sophisticated lamps that we found ourselves enjoying from time to time. They included lanterns for times of crisis in the farmyard.

- There was something special about the Christmas candles and also about the blessed candles associated with Baptism and the 'Last Rites'. These were kept in a special drawer.

When I went home after my ordination, all was changed. The big topic of conversation was rural electrification. The River Lee was showing resources that we had never dreamt of. A small number of people resisted this revolution of light, but there was no going back. As I reflect on it all now, I would say that one of the greatest human developments in my lifetime was in the new ways in which we have come to understand and appreciate words like 'lamp' and 'light'. The countless new forms of lighting have given us new entry into multiple forms of darkness, multiple areas of the unknown, multiple areas of ignorance and superstition.

Let there be light
The world of both the Old and New Testaments was certainly the pre-electrification world. It was the world of the equivalents of paraffin lamps, tilly lamps, lanterns and candles.

- It is in such a world that Jesus spoke about the girls who begged for oil because their lamps were going out (Mt 25:8), about letting our lights shine (Mt 5:16), and indeed about his own being the light of the world (Jn 8:12).

- It was also a world in which there was a special appreciation of the light that comes from sun, moon and stars.

- The shaping of these light-givers had been a special stage in the accounts of creation in the first pages of the Bible. Before this was darkness, a darkness that we now know is likely to return when our planet has completed its lifespan.

- Sun, moon and stars feature in the great vision of the triumphant church in the Book of Revelation: 'A woman clothed with the sun, with the moon under her feet and on her head a crown of twelve stars' (Rev 12:1). In the Catholic tradition, the vision has provided an approach to Mary in the language of stars. It has been the inspiration for images as diverse as the Miraculous Medal and the EU flag.

Looking towards the sun, the moon and the stars provided light and hope for many in the biblical world.

- The father of John the Baptist welcomed God's tender mercy coming as the dawn from on high (Lk 1:78).

- In drawing attention to the word of the prophets, the author of 2 Peter invited his readers to look to the 'lamp shining in a dark place, until the day dawns and the morning star rises in your hearts' (1:19).

- In that perspective, it is easy to see how Jesus came to be understood as 'Morning Star' (Rev 22:16) and 'Sun of Justice' (Litany of the Holy Name). The sun image, in turn, gave rise to the attitude of regarding facing towards the east as the ideal setting for Christian churches.

- Describing Mary by such titles as 'Morning Star' and 'Star of the Sea' arose out of an appreciation of the unique way she was enlightened in her relationship with her Son.

Walking in the light

The Book of Revelation says that in the glory of heaven there will be no need of sun or moon to shine on it, for the glory of God is its light and its lamp is the Lamb (21:23). We are being told that Jesus Christ in glory will be incomparably greater than the created sun and moon. The lamp that is the Lamb will have none of the limitations of even the great lamps that God made at the dawning of creation. This must have provided a language of hope for a people who had to live in the darkness of the new 'Babylonian captivity' that was the background for the Book of Revelation. The nastier side of the Roman Empire, notably in the destruction of the temple, was providing a continual and bitter reminder of the devastation brought about by earlier empires.

It is in this context that I like to see Pope John Paul II's introducing of the 'Mysteries of Light' into the Rosary.

- He knew that we get much light from the joyful, sorrowful and glorious mysteries. His desire was to show us that Jesus, the one light of the world, keeps beaming his light on us from every stage of his public ministry as well.

- *The Baptism of Jesus* throws light on all the ways we

need to be continually reborn of water and the Holy Spirit (cf Jn 3:5).

- *The wedding at Cana* throws light on all our marriages, all our feasts, all our need to experience the new wine in the new wineskins of the gospel (Jn 2:1 ff; cf Mt 9:17).

- *The proclaiming of the kingdom of God* highlights the programme of the kingdom that is the Beatitudes (Mt 5:1-12) and the related call to let our lights shine (Mt 5:14).

- *The transfiguration of Jesus* shows his face lighting up as he hears the reassuring words of the Father preparing him for and making sense of his suffering (Mt 17:2).

- *The Last Supper* is the high point of the many meals which he shared with a great variety of people.

The Mysteries of Light help me to appreciate a beautiful page in Judy Coyne's book. She tells us how the best known witness of the apparition, Mrs O'Connell, said that all the figures were 'made of light' but that the brightest light came from the Lamb. As I journey in prayer through the Mysteries of Light, I thank God for the great riches in each of them rather than wish that I knew more about the public life of Jesus.

States of light
My own tradition of spirituality owes a lot to the seventeenth century 'French School' by which St Vincent de Paul was much influenced. The most prominent

members of the school had much to say about our call to identify with each of the 'states' of Christ, from his helplessness in the womb and in the manger to his present state of glory, at the right hand of his Father.

- The spirituality distilled from these states consists of a readiness to follow Jesus Christ, with faith and devotion, and to adhere to him from one state to the next.

- This readiness can cause us many a jolt. It can involve a continual uprooting that can upset us when we prefer to say 'it is good for us to stay in this place' and to set up a lasting dwelling rather than to move on (cf Lk 9:33).

- The readiness was well captured by Blessed Columba Marmion, especially in his *Christ in his Mysteries.*

- The same readiness helps me to move from one of the twenty mysteries of the Rosary to the next.

- Each of Christ's many mysteries is a mystery of light. Each of them points to a 'state' of Christ, and his call to me to join in it, sometimes at a very short notice.

Feasts of Light
With Christ as our Morning Star, and in the company of all the 'stars' that comprise the communion of saints, it is not surprising that the church has many feasts of light.

- At Christmas we celebrate the light coming into

the world for those who sit in darkness (Lk 1:79). On the night of the birth of the light of the world, the heavens were lit up and a glorious light surrounded the shepherds (Lk 2:9).

- Some days later, the Magi from the east followed the star that came to shine where our 'Morning Star' was (Mt 2:9). No wonder that the twelve days of Christmas are a time of lighting candles.

- Forty days after Christmas, we have Candlemas Day. The star of that day is the old man Simeon who recognised Christ as the light for revelation to the Gentiles (Lk 2:32).

- Our greatest feast of light is Easter. We light our candles from the great Easter candle which is Christ. The Easter Candle continues to stay lighting for the whole of the Easter season.

- The spirit of all the great feasts of light overflows into the practice of the prayerful lighting of candles in churches and in the candlelight processions in places like Lourdes. The recent moves towards having similar processions in Knock have roots in the early history of the shrine.

- The celebration of light is well captured in the Lucernarium with which some Christian communities celebrate first Vespers on Saturday evening, in preparation for the glory of Sunday morning. It can be a splendid setting for singing Cardinal Newman's 'Lead kindly light, amid the encircling gloom.'

Two helps
Over the past half century we have received many helps to recognise Jesus as the Lamb of God, lighting up our darkness on the way to our final abode where there will no longer be need for the light of sun, moon and stars. Two of them deserve special attention. The first was in a great invitation to the whole church to follow Jesus Christ, the light of all nations.

- The Constitition *Light of Nations* is one of the great foundation documents of the Second Vatican Council.

- Its authors looked at many possible approaches to an understanding of the church.

- They eventually decided on two introductory chapters on *The Mystery of the Church* and *The People of God*.

- The first of the eight chapters leads up to Jesus the light of all peoples. It sets the tone for the other chapters.

- In the course of the second chapter, our attention is drawn to the many ways in which the new People of God are united with Christ the light.

- The succeeding chapters describe the mystery, the secret but unfolding plan of God being worked out on every level of the pilgrim church's daily life and ministry. The baptismal call to holiness is seen as going out to all – married, single or in consecrated virginity.

- The final chapter presents Mary as embodying all the aspirations to holiness contained in the earlier chapters and as playing a uniquely active part in the communion of saints. Mary keeps pointing to the great light that keeps enlightening everybody (cf Jn 1:9).

A second help to recognise Jesus as the light is a growing appreciation of the works of St John of the Cross, the saint of 'the dark night of the soul'. When I began my seminary studies, I looked on this great lover as a man living in 'unapproachable light', with a message only for those in the rarefied world of the mystics.

- When I read Roy Campbell's translation of his poems shortly after its publication in 1951, I found myself saying 'This is for me; this is for all of us!'

- I discovered that John's rather dense prose works are mostly commentaries on his wonderful poems.

- I discovered that he is not only the saint of the dark night but the saint who described himself as 'with no other light except for that which in my heart was burning'.

- I discovered that it is in the darkness we can often best appreciate the light.

- I rediscovered a truth dear to many Christian mystics: that the biblical 'cloud by day' was a symbol of God's presence, not of God's absence.

After all the years, my favourite lines from the Roy

Campbell translations are 'O night that was my guide! O darkness dearer than the morning's pride', and the refrain 'Although by night … though it was night … for it is night' in the 'Song of the Soul that is glad to know God by faith'. I got a lot of light from the Letter of Pope John Paul II for the fourth centenary of the death of John of the Cross in 1990. In the writings of the saint, he pointed to many shafts of light for today's darkness.

Light and love
During the early months of his papacy, we all wondered what would be the topic for Pope Benedict XVI's first encyclical. Some people were surprised and many were delighted when he eventually reminded the whole world that God is Love.

- The encyclical helps us to see the Trinity as a kind of reservoir for all love;

- to see creation as an overflowing of the reservoir;

- to see the Incarnation as the seeping of God's infinite love into all human flesh, as the Word made flesh invites us to be one body, one spirit in him;

- to see the end of the world as the final victory of love over all the darkness that we experience.

A very short time before the publication of the encyclical, Pope Benedict said that 'Light and love are the same reality.' They are, he said, 'the primordial creative power that moves the universe.' He went on to say that the wonder of the gospel is that 'God the infinite light has a human face and, we may add, a human heart.' In this spirit, the theme for all Lourdes pilgrimages in 2006 was 'Keep your lamps lit'. It was an invitation to keep lighting our lamps from the lamp that is the Lamb.

Jesus has told us how to deal with one day's darkness at a time (cf Mt 6:34). Every day, he himself comes to us like the dawn from on high (cf Lk 1:78). As a result, no day can be entirely dark.

Reflection Five

Washed White in the Lamb's Blood (Rev 7:14)

On Holy Saturday night, the presiding priest traces the first letter of the Greek alphabet over the cross on the Paschal candle:

- He traces the last letter of the alphabet below the cross;
- He traces the numerals of the present year between the arms of the cross;
- When the accompanying prayer is ended, he can choose to insert five grains of incense into the candle and pray 'by his holy and glorious wounds, may Christ our Lord guard us and keep us';
- He lights the candle from the new fire, saying 'May the light of Christ, rising in glory, dispel the darkness of our hearts and minds.'

The holy and glorious wounds of Christ are the wounds out of which came his life-blood, the blood of the new covenant of which he is the agent (cf Heb 9: 15). In the biblical tradition, there is a special connection between the shedding of blood in sacrifice and the remission of sins (Heb 9:22). The life-giving blood coming from Our Lord's wounds, and celebrated in the sorrowful mysteries of the Rosary, keeps spilling into the joyful mysteries, the glorious mysteries, and the mysteries of light. The transformed wounds of Jesus give limitless value to his intercession for us at the Father's right hand (Heb 7:25). They are the perfect incense of praise and worship that continually rises up to the Father in heaven.

The bleeding wounds of the body of Christ have been reflected in the whole church at every stage of her history:

- The saints have at all times been willing to identify with these wounds and to 'carry the marks of Jesus' in their bodies (cf Gal 6:17);

- When St Pio of Pietrelcina carried them in a literal way, the whole church looked on in wonder;

- There is no doubt that our generation has had its own share in the weakness and wounds of Christ;

- Indeed it could be said that Christ's church was never so much seen to be wounded as it is today;

- We are all entering painfully into the five 'holy and glorious wounds' by which our Saviour wishes to 'guard and keep us';

- This is God's saving way of continually turning bad news into good news;

- By the power of the holy and glorious wounds of our Saviour, our new wounds are continually put into saving touch with the holiness and glory of God. The holiness of God is God's totally perfect and limitless way of existing, of knowing and of loving. The glory of God is the shining forth among us of that holiness.

Many wounds

Over the centuries, the most accepted way of naming the five wounds of Christ has been in terms of the head, each of the hands, the feet nailed together, the side.

Wounds in the head: The wounded head of Christ has an urgent message today for those who have received the sacrament of Ordination:

- At Ordination, priests receive a special sharing in the headship of Christ;

- Like the headship of Christ, their headship calls them to be leaders and to be life-giving;

- As wounded healers, they are, sometimes with great pain, coming to realise that they need to depend on a power greater than themselves. This power resides in the head of Christ who is the only head of the church (cf Col 1:18).

Wounds in the hands: Two of the five wounds of Christ were in his hands:

- These were the hands that tenderly took the restored-to-life child and gave him to his mother (Lk 7:15);

- They were the hands that touched the hands of Peter's mother-in-law (Mt 8:15);

- They were the hands that took the little daughter of Jairus by the hand (Mk 5:41);

- They were the hands that continually blessed;

- They were the hands that, in a special kind of blessing, took the eucharistic bread and cup (Lk 22:17-23);

- They were the hands that healed and gave life, in a whole range of healings;

- They were the hands that, at the Ascension, were lifted up in blessing (Lk 24:50).

The disciple who was the author of 1 John was proud that his own hands had touched what was from the beginning (1 Jn 1:1).

Following the whole range of movements of the hands of Jesus, and joining our hands with his hands, is a programme for all women and men who serve and minister in the church. It is a programme of touching what was from the beginning, of keeping in living touch with the glorified wounds of Christ.

Wounds in the feet: The wounds of the hands of Jesus are closely linked with the wounds in his feet:

- In his risen appearances, he showed both hands and feet to his disciples (Lk 24:39, 40);

- His short public ministry had been a time of many journeys, many walkings;

- He knew what it was to have tired feet (Jn 4:6);

- His whole message was an invitation to walk not in darkness but in the light (Jn 8:12);

- The missionary walkings of Jesus reached a high

point when he began to wash his disciples' feet (Jn 13:5). Peter's astonished reaction elicited from Jesus a programme and a style for all who would serve in the church (vv 12ff). It called for a continual washing of feet, hands and head. This message got a new poignancy when the feet of Jesus himself were nailed to the cross, after a trying journey on foot.

Wound in the side: The account of the opening of the side of Jesus (Jn 19:34) evokes the whole mystery of the blood of the new covenant as well as of the water of Baptism coming from the side of the new temple which is Christ's body (cf Jn 7:37, 38).

It also provides continually new perspectives on the mysterious union between man and woman that started in the side of the first Adam and that keeps coming alive in the mystery of Christ and his church (cf Eph 5:32).

The blood we call precious
The opened side of Jesus is a kind of shorthand for his whole mission and ministry. It is only in all of his holy and glorious wounds that the church today will find its real strength. We belong to a church wounded by failures in faith, in hope, in love, in mercy, in fidelity. We are consoled as we remember that, over the centuries, Christians have expressed special affection for and devotion to the precious blood coming from the holy and glorious wounds:

• The First Letter of Peter laid a rich foundation for

this devotion. 'You were ransomed,' it says, 'not with perishable things like silver and gold, but with the precious blood of Christ, like that of a lamb without defect or blemish' (1 Pet 1:18, 19);

- St Catherine of Siena's experience in the depths of her prayer contributed much to the spreading and deepening of the devotion;

- With the initiative of Pope John XXIII, the invocation 'blessed be his most precious blood' found a place in the divine praises at Benediction;

- The martyrs were always seen as throwing special light on the meaning of the precious blood;

- Their own blood was described as the seed of Christians;

- The oldest extant homily in the Irish language, on the margin of a seventh or eighth century manuscript in Cambrai, pointed out that there are three kinds of martyrdom: the white martyrdom of parting and exile; the green (blue) martyrdom of self-control and fasting; the red martyrdom of destruction and death. I believe that the descriptions are deliberately vague to leave space for the multiple ways in which we can all be immersed in the precious blood coming from the holy and glorious wounds of Christ. Only these can give meaning and energy to all Christian martyrdom.

Praying on the topic of the holy and glorious wounds encouraged devout believers to compose prayers like the well-known 'I kiss the wounds of your sacred head ... your sacred hands ... your sacred side ... your sacred feet ... May every step I walk today be an act of love for you';

- In our devotional prayers, the only time we ask to get drunk is when we say 'Blood of Christ inebriate me';

- In the same breath, we ask the water from the side of Christ to wash us, the passion of Christ to strengthen us, the wounds of Christ to hide us.

Washing white with Christ's blood
Those of us who minister at the Knock shrine see a special message in the fact that, in the language of the Book of Revelation (Rev 5:11-14), the Lamb is both slain and victorious. He is the Lamb who came to take away the sin and the sins of all the world. Is it any wonder that the ministry of reconciliation is so central at the shrine? At a time when appreciation of the sacrament is at a crossroads, we have a daily opportunity to keep pointing to the mission of the Lamb as experienced by John the Baptist. Within the framework of the church's revised *Rite of Penance*, we have scope for many creative ways of telling people that, by the strength of the Lamb's precious blood, their sins are being taken away and their 'transgressions are being blotted out' by the abundant mercy of God (cf Ps 51).

Losing a sense of sin?
It is often said that people today have lost a sense of sin. One should not rush to say yes or no to this contention.

- It is certain that sin is a reality;

- It is also certain that the all-holy God abhors sin and that his Son, our Saviour, came to take away sin and help people to experience the infinite mercy and holiness of the Father;

- Praying at Knock helps to put sin in perspective;

- It helps us to see what is really sinful and what is merely an expression of our human limitations and frailty;

- The Knock apparition was a great expression of the holiness of God;

- It revealed the Lamb of God who, because he alone is holy, wishes to take away whatever is unholy and to keep washing us white with his blood;

- The fifteen witnesses saw the woman who is both holy mother of God and refuge of sinners;

- Along with her were two key members of the communion of saints, the holy ones;

- All those who minister at Knock help people to experience the holiness of God which keeps overflowing into all the communion of saints;

- There will be no re-discovery of the sense of sin

until people re-discover the holiness of God. But, as we come to re-discover that holiness, we hasten to have our sins washed away. We are here at the heart of the daily mission of Knock.

Pilgrims at Knock sometimes stop a priest and ask 'are you hearing today, father?' It is a thought pro-voking question. I pray that every priest in the Knock ministry will be a good hearer and a good listener to what God is asking us all to do in the re-shaping of the sacrament of reconciliation with the all-holy God.

The paradox of blood

When we talk of the red blood of the Son of God that washes us white from our sins we are right into the world of paradox;

- Blood is a friendly word;

- We are proud of those who are our blood-relatives, our kith and kin;

- We are happy to give a blood transfusion, a life transfusion;

- We are relieved when we learn that all our blood tests are positive;

- We are inspired by the edifying legend of the peli-can nurturing her own young with her blood;

- And yet, blood can be a horrendous word. Are there any more off-putting words than bloodshed, blood-stained, blood-curdling, blood-thirsty?

- The paradox of the blood of Christ is that in the

depths of his humiliation his wounds became holy and glorious;

- As a result, the Lamb of God has washed us white with his blood (Rev 7:14);

- To paraphrase Ps 51, we can say that the red blood of Christ washes us whiter than snow (v 7).

One of the great hymns of the church sings of the white-robed army of martyrs. Truly the distinctive colours of the church are red and white! The two colours keep helping us to cope with life's paradoxes, life's contradictions, life's absurdities.

A debasing of martyrdom?
Some recent events have tended to debase the Christian ideal of martyrdom;

- We have been hearing of suicide bombing;

- We have been hearing of new forms of bondage and ransoming in ways that bring out the more depressing aspects of blood words;

- We are getting many reminders that all human bloodshed, including the shedding of the blood of Christ, is monstrous;

- We find ourselves in agreement with the woman in *The Playboy of the Western World* who, after an initial infatuation, came to see clearly that there is a big difference between a romantic tale of bloodshed and a dastardly deed in your back garden.

The celebrations in Ireland of the nineteeth anniversary of the 1916 Rising have given many people second thoughts about the mystique of bloodshed;

- I myself have been having mixed feelings about the blood language in the song about the ambush in my native parish of Kilmichael;

- Even the story of Pádraig Pearse, who for so long was presented as an icon of noble and innocent love of country, has been under new scrutiny;

- Many people are finding themselves nodding approval at the views of a much-respected Jesuit scholar in an article that was written for the fiftieth anniversary of the 1916 Rising but that was refused publication until there was a lot of bloodshed in the North of Ireland. He said very directly that Pearse's equation of Calvary with the republicans' giving of their lives was nothing less than blasphemous;

- There have been many other re-assessments of the language of blood as used in connection with 1916;

- Certainly men like Joseph Mary Plunkett, who saw Christ's blood on the rose, were people of very noble aspirations;

- Their idealism was in some way related to the one that made countless men ready to lay down their lives in the first world war;

- Debate will continue about the diverse elements that went into the making of all this idealism. These include many human limitations.

A unique bloodshed

As we reflect on the giving and shedding of blood, in the noblest and least noble senses, we are led to thank God for the unique sacrifice of his beloved Son;

- There is a sense in which the shedding of blood is the essence of the best of sacrifice (cf Heb 9:22);

- There is an important sense in which it isn't;

- We continue to get hope from the blood of the Lamb that washes us white;

- We continue to reverence the blood of Christ and to pray that it will be 'blessed';

- But our disillusionment with anything that smacks of violence has led us to seek anew for the essence of sacrifice;

- As we re-read Psalm 51, we learn that God takes no delight in any sacrifice that is not from the heart;

- As we listen again to God speaking through the prophet Amos, we see more clearly that he takes no pleasure in holocausts, oblations and sacrifices of fattened cattle (5:21-23).

- From these and similar sources, we learn that God never takes delight in the shedding of blood as such; it is not in the knife of their destruction and the shedding of their blood that he is pleased with victims;

- The whole of the Letter to the Hebrews makes it clear that Jesus identified with the sentiments expressed in Psalm 40: Sacrifice and offering you do not desire, but you have given me an open ear ... Then I said 'Here I am ... I delight to do your will, O my God; your law is within my heart' (vv 6-8).

Our emphasis today has moved away from placing the essence of sacrifice in the shedding of blood;

- The words in the Letter to the Hebrews about their being no remission of sin without the shedding of blood (Heb 9:22) get their real meaning in the unique sacrifice of Jesus Christ;

- The essence of sacrifice is in a human heart reaching out in love into the heart of God and in the readiness to give everything one has;

- The message of Calvary is that this is precisely what Jesus did. Doing it cost him the last drop of his blood in a violent and totally undeserved death. This is why we continue to 'bless' God for this precious blood. We are really blessing the heart from which it came.

In his first encyclical, Pope Benedict XVI kept inviting us to reach into the pierced side of Christ and to be in touch with his blood poured out in the love than which no love can be greater. It is a new invitation to appreciate the heart we call sacred.

Reflection Six

Jesus both Lamb and Lion

If they were asked what do lambs and lions have in common, most people would say that there is very little, if anything. Their image of the lamb may come from the popular poem: 'All in the April evening ... I thought of the Lamb of God going meekly to die'. The lion, on the other hand, is seen as anything but meek. The lion is fierce. The lion roars. Lions hunt for their prey. Lions devour. Lions tend to tear their prey to pieces. In a popular nursery rhyme, the lion is fighting with the unicorn and beating the unicorn all around the town.

The Bible, for the most part, shares in the popular perceptions about the lion.

- The lion's roar makes people afraid (Amos 3:8);

- The lion is sometimes paired with the serpent; if you dwell in the shelter of the Most High you will do the impossible; you will trample both of them under foot (Ps 91:13);

- The story of Daniel in the den (Dan 6) is not complimentary towards lions;

- In the New Testament, the most scathing words said about the lion are in the First Letter of Peter, in a text highlighted in the *Prayer of the Church*. The readers are warned of the need to discipline themselves and remain alert because, like a roaring lion, their adversary the Devil prowls around, looking for someone to devour. He is to be resisted, with steadfast faith;

• The Letter makes it clear that the threat of being devoured is not confined to one place; believers everywhere are undergoing the same kind of suffering (1 Pet 5:7-9).

And still, the lion was not totally bad news:

• The lion is strong; the lion has a majestic and attractive figure;

• The righteous (Prov 28:1), some prophets (Jer 2:3) and even God himself (Hos 13:7) had qualities that were reminders of the lion;

• When Jacob wanted to find words to praise the son of whom he was most proud and from whom people would boast of their descent, he drew liberally on the image of the lion:
'Judah, your brothers shall praise you;
Your hand shall be on the neck of your enemies;
Your father's sons shall bow down before you.

Judah is a lion's whelp;
From the prey, my son, you have gone up.

He crouches down, he stretches out like a lion.

The scepter shall not depart from Judah,

Nor the ruler's staff from beneath his feet, until he comes to whom it belongs;
And the obedience of the peoples is his (Gen 49:8-10)'.

• It is significant that, after many readings from Isaiah during the Advent season, these prophetic words get a prominent place in the church's liturgy of 17 December, just a week before we celebrate the birth of the Messiah.

The lion of the tribe of Judah
As a fulfilling of Jacob's strong aspirations, the Book of Revelation presents the Lamb and the Lion of the tribe of Judah not just as related but as identical (Rev 5:5);

• This is the perfect harmonising of opposites, the perfect paradox;

• Is it any wonder that, with the advance of the Christian centuries, Leo became a popular Christian name and a name chosen by many popes?

• The fact that, in the person of Jesus, the qualities of both lamb and lion can exist together has many implications;

• Seeing Jesus as the meek and mild lamb can lead us to preach and teach a rather one-dimensional, innocuous Saviour and to close our eyes to the aspects of Jesus that make him more resemble the lion;

• Think of his 'woes' that follow immediately on the Beatitudes (Lk 6:24-26);

- Think of his cleansing of the temple, as he makes whips to clear out whatever made his Father's house more like a den of robbers than a house of prayer (Lk 19:45, 46);

- Think of his cutting description of Herod as 'that fox' (Lk 13:32);

- Think of his condemnation of the scribes and Pharisees and of hypocrisy in all its forms (e.g. Mt 23:23-36).

Yes, Jesus showed some of the characteristics of the lion;

- He also likened himself to some people who are not high up on the honours lists;

- As well as telling us that he is the 'Good Shepherd' (Jn 10:11), he made it clear that he is also the good burglar. When he was accused of driving out Satan by the power of Beelzebub, a charge that was the exact opposite of all he stood for, he replied: 'When a strong man, fully armed, guards his castle, his property is safe. But when one stronger than he attacks him and overpowers him, he takes away his armour in which he trusted, and divides his plunder (Lk 11:21, 22)'.

I once led a day of recollection in London for a group of priest chaplains. I preached on the theme of Jesus the good burglar. A priest thanked me afterwards and told me that he was chaplain to a large prison. He added that he wouldn't be preaching on the burglar theme on the following Sunday! He was very wise but our conversation deepened in me the wish that the 'boundless riches of Christ' (Eph 3:8) will be more and more opened up as the word of God is proclaimed.

The lion of Narnia

A feature of some very successful fictional writing in recent years has been that the world of some authors is inhabited by humans and by a variety of other known and unknown animals. It is one more expression of Pope Gregory's teaching that the whole of creation is in each of us;

- Sometimes we can name our affinities with other animals and with the rest of creation;

- Sometimes we are helped by literary and other artists;

- One cannot but get many religious insights from reading J. R. R. Tolkien's *Silmarillion*, peopled by hobbits, elves, wizards and dwarves. Here you are dealing with more than fiction. You are in touch with a redemptive message coming from Tolkien's Christian worldview;

- The same can be said of the writings of C. S. Lewis, as he introduces us to the world of his Narnia books. In *The Lion, the Witch and the Wardrobe*, we find four children passing through the wardrobe of ordinary living into the wintry world of Narnia;

- Narnia is a world of talking beasts;

- The white witch has cursed the land with eternal winter; Aslan, the lion, is the king and god of Narnia;

- He has been overthrown by the white witch;

- Amazingly, against all that we might expect from lions, he later sacrifices his life, to atone for all that has gone wrong. As the fruit of his sacrifice, he is resurrected and he restores spring to Narnia. This is not the roaring, devouring lion. It is the tamed lion longed for by Isaiah in another Advent reading (11:6, 7).

There were many explanations of the story. A recently-discovered letter of Lewis removed all confusion. He thought the redeeming figure would become a lion in Narnia, as he became a man here. Why his choice of animal? The lion, said Lewis, with all his faults, is widely acknowledged as the king of the beasts. To set this in the biblical and Christian context, Lewis envisaged the Narnia lion as the lion of the tribe of Judah. The whole story has many messages of hope. It is a powerful expression of how the winter of our discontent can often have the makings of spring. It provides a reason of further exploring the implications of St Mark's simple statement that, at the time of his testing, Jesus was 'with the wild beasts' (1:13).

The taming of the lion
Fr Raymond Brown, who opened up the scriptures for so many people, used to ask himself publicly what are the most consoling words in the whole New Testament;

- Without any hesitation he always answered that they are the words of Jesus inviting us to come to him (Mt 11:28-30);

- The invitation is given to all who are weary and carrying heavy burdens;

- They are invited to carry the easy yoke of his plough, to carry his light burden and, above all, to learn from him for he is meek and humble of heart, and they will find rest for their souls;

- The words follow immediately on the secret told by Jesus that no one knows the Father except the Son and anyone to whom the Son chooses to reveal him (v 27).

Jesus invites us to learn from him precisely because he is gentle and humble. The more familiar translation says 'meek and humble'. I believe that a continual exploring of these two words will help us to see how Jesus was, at the same time, both Lamb and Lion;

- William Barclay, that great searcher into gospel words, pointed out that behind the meek-gentle language of the gospel there are two very different worlds;

- One is the world of the humble, lowly ones, the *anawim* of whom Mary is the flowering;

- The second, very surprisingly, is the world of the taming of wild animals;

- Seen against this background, the meek people are

the tamed people. The meek person is so 'tamed' that he or she has both gentleness and strength of steel, with all their drives under control.

- William Barclay sees the 'tamed' person as God-controlled; only God can give the 'untamed' person the perfect mastery; only God can tame us;

- The God who tames us doesn't annihilate our anger;

- He helps us get it into focus; this focusing seems to be more difficult for some of us than for others;

- There was a time when anger was seen simply as a sin to be confessed. Today people are ready to own their anger in a way that seems almost entirely new. People are saying 'I am angry with God.' This usually happens when they are faced with the great 'why-oh-why?' questions, the kind that tortured Job and made him give strong expression to all his emotions, including being angry with God. It is often good to tell such people that they needn't worry. God can take it!;

- Which brings us to the anger of Jesus. It was the anger he showed when he gave expression to his lion qualities;

- With all reverence, one might ask whether some of the years spent prior to his public ministry were spent 'taming', but not destroying, some of the lion qualities in him;

- As he grew in taming, he grew in humility, that

virtue that makes us realise that we are very much of the earth but that we are constantly being lifted up to the heavens to be one family with the princes of God's people (cf Ps 113:8).

Two saints of tameness
When St Vincent de Paul founded his community of priests and brothers of the Mission, he named five virtues by which they would be especially distinguished; two of them are meekness and humility. In the light of William Barclay's words, I have come to call them taming and humility. With the strong foundation of these virtues, he asked his brethren to live lives of gospel simplicity, mortification and zeal;

- He presented meekness in terms of help to practise pastoral zeal wherever there are excesses in areas like religious conflicts, drunkenness, sexual disorder, ambition;

- He knew that this called for daily mortification, a continual dying to selfishness;

- He openly expressed regret for the three times in his life when he was lacking in meekness;

- He saw a special urgency for the need of meekness in the practice of what we today call ecumenical dialogue.

In all his search for a growth in meekness, he looked to his mentor, St Francis de Sales; for Francis himself, the taming hadn't always been easy.

Drinking the cup that tames
Jesus described the brothers James and John as 'sons of thunder' (Mk 3:17). To tame their thundering and their ambition for power, he later asked them were they able to drink his cup (Mk 10:38);

• Every disciple of Jesus is asked to drink many cups along life's journey: the cup of joy, the bitter cup, the cup of blessing. They all help to tame us in whatever lion qualities are not of the Lamb of God;

• As we learn from our one Teacher who is meek and humble of heart, he introduces us into the mystery of the Father and of the Son and of the Spirit who unites Father and Son;

• With the help of the visual aid of Rublev's great icon, we continually sit at the eucharistic table of Father, Son and Spirit and drink from their cup as they wish to drink from ours (cf Rev 3:20). In the strength of that cup, we are enabled to drink the bitter cups of life as well as the cups that cheer. This is Christian taming in daily action.

Reflection Seven

Bringing the Multitudes before the Lamb (Rev 7)

In the promise that God made to him, Abraham was assured that his descendants would be as numerous as the stars of heaven and the sands on the seashore (Gen 22:17). Any attempt to do this counting would boggle the greatest of human imaginations;

- The descendants of Abraham are those who identify with him in his faith;

- In the Letter to the Hebrews, the faith of Abraham is highly praised;

- Along with him are praised a large diversity of people;

- The inclusion of some of them is quite surprising;

- As we read the list, we find ourselves re-assessing the criteria for recognising men and women of faith (Heb 11:8 ff).

- From the Christian point of view, the faith of Abraham has been transmuted into faith in Jesus Christ in whom all salvation is concentrated (Acts 4:12).

The Book of Revelation (ch. 7: 4 ff) provides a great vision of those who will be sealed with the seal of

God's approval and will be part of the new heaven and the new earth (cf 21:1-3).

• The man who had this great vision, at Patmos, tells us that his name was John (Rev 1:9). He shares more than a name with the St John of the Knock apparition. He saw 144,000 people who bore the seal of God's approval and stood before the victorious Lamb. There were 12,000 from each of the twelve tribes of Israel. The number is obviously symbolic. There is no hint as to how many will finally be saved.

• The vision of those sealed from the twelve tribes is immediately followed by a vision of a great number that nobody could count, from all tribes and peoples and languages.

• When we reflect on this great vision of salvation, we realise that the biggest of our calculations wouldn't fit into even a tiny section of any sands near the smallest of seas.

• The great prayer of praise of the countless people saved is a salutary reminder that we are not our own saviours. 'Salvation,' we are told, 'belongs to our God who is seated on the throne, and to the Lamb' (Rev 7:10).

Numbers, numbers and numbers
And still, we are all fascinated by numbers;

• Whether we admit it or not, we like to boast about an increase in numbers in the works with which we are associated;

- We love to see full churches;

- We are happy to talk about an increase in numbers at our shrines and places of pilgrimage;

- We are delighted when we have to search for extra chairs when big numbers turn up in the community centre;

- All this can be very gratifying but, where true gospel values are concerned, 'how many?' is not the most important question;

- We like to ask 'How many?' and 'When?' The gospel is more interested in 'What kind of person?' and 'How?';

- When he was asked how many will be saved, Jesus didn't answer the question; he told the questioner to enter by the narrow gate (Lk 13:23, 24);

- He was similarly asked when the end would be and what would be the signs of his coming; again, he refused to give an answer;

- The focus of all the teaching of Jesus was on what kind of person will enter the kingdom of heaven and how one can become such a person. He emphasised the great importance of being ready; what he said to his questioner he said to all: 'Keep awake' (Mk 13:37);

- Like the visionary in the Book of Revelation, Jesus made it clear that all salvation is the gift of God; he also made it clear that we must keep awake and freely co-operate with this gift. To those who wondered how this was possible, he said 'You know neither the scriptures nor the power of God' (Mt 22:29).

One thing is clear. It is God's wish that all will be saved (1 Tim 2:4);

- But salvation is not to be presumed;

- In his command to go out and make disciples of all nations, Jesus told us that those who believe and are baptised will be saved and that those who refuse to believe will be condemned (Mk 16:16). This is the kind of message that makes us ask many questions about 'How?' and 'What kind of person?', rather than about 'How many?' and 'When?';

In my lifetime as a priest, I have been led to see all four questions from a variety of perspectives. I began my priestly ministry with a very literal and exclusivist understanding of words that for many centuries held a prominent place in Catholic teaching: 'Outside the church there is no salvation';

- I was ordained into a very missionary church;

- From Ireland alone, several missionaries went out, literally, to the whole world;

- Some went to those already believing in Christ;

- Some went to bring the good news where it hadn't been preached before;

- Born and reared in a place where there was a very

high rate of religious practice, I could make a good estimate of those who believed and were baptised;

- I envied St Paul in his assurance that the gospel was growing in the whole world (Col 1:6). I knew that there were sections of the world which the gospel had not yet reached;

- But I was confident that the God of mercy would find a way of saving the people in such outer regions;

- I was sharing in the optimism of a church that seemed to be making continual headway and that was planting new mustard seeds (cf Mk 4:31) even in parts of the world that were, in many ways, new.

Changing perspectives
Over the years, my perspectives have been changing all the time;

- There are now over six billion people on our planet;

- About one billion of these or more are Catholic Christians;

- It would appear that, even if we are just only to hold our own relative to world population, we would need to multiply our conversion rate very considerably;

- A more disturbing question concerns the criteria we use to calculate the numbers of Catholic believers;

- We are told that about fifty per cent of Irish Catholics are 'practising'. But in what sense practising?;

- In the Irish census of 2006, all were asked to declare their religion. A small number of religions were listed and a space was left for each correspondent to fill. I am sure that quite a few people who felt they were on the periphery wondered how to answer;

- There seem to be a large number of people today to whom the words of the psalmist would apply: 'Fools say in their hearts, There is no God' (Ps 14: 1); The psalmist was not speaking about militant atheists; there was question more of those who live as if God didn't exist;

- This situation of practical atheism could be multiplied umpteen times over in the rest of the world's six billions.

Indications are that the situation will worsen further;

- We have been hearing many sombre predictions;

- There are suggestions that, in some places where a strong Catholic presence has been taken for granted, the situation will change utterly within a small number of generations;

- In the meantime, in most of the traditionally Catholic countries, the number of people taking part in the Sunday Eucharist is diminishing, dramatically so in some countries;

- There has been a closing down of many Catholic landmark institutions;

- There has been a big decline in vocations to priesthood and religious life;

- To say that this is just a European and North American phenomenon is to over-simplify;

- One wishes well to the oft-named countries where there is a super-abundance of vocations but, in these countries too, there are cultural and social changes. Vocation is certainly a call and a grace from God. But the call and the grace are incarnated in a particular cultural and social setting. One hopes that the countries that at present are experiencing 'seven years of plenty' will learn from those of us who are now experiencing 'seven years of famine' (cf Gen 41/27ff).

Of course, predictions can be wrong. In the seventeenth century, St Vincent de Paul seemed convinced that, in the not too distant future, the church in France would be in its death-throes. It is true that, three and a half centuries on, the majority of French people seem to live without any consciousness of the reality of God. But the church in France is producing many seeds of new life. Some of them are growing in communities with inspiring names like 'Emmanuel' and 'Beatitudes'. Who can predict what will be the final flowering of such lovely seeds?

God's saving grace at work
So, with all the new perspectives on salvation, are we simply left with several unanswered questions? To this I would say a definite no!

• As the years go on, I am coming to realise more and more that Jesus Christ is the only Saviour of all people. But, rather than say 'outside the church there is no salvation', I find myself saying 'without Jesus Christ …
  - without the community who believe in him and give witness to all he stands for …
  - without those who serve all people in his name …
  - without the communities who celebrate the Eucharist and all it stands for …
  - without the communion of saints of which the church is a privileged part …
  - there is no salvation.'

Instead of speaking of the Catholic Church as the 'one, true church', I believe that, in the words of the Second Vatican Council, the one church of Christ 'subsists in' the Catholic Church. This encourages me to see the grace of Christ at work in other 'churches and ecclesial communities'. And instead of denying the action of God's saving grace in people of other religions, I say, again in the words of the Second Vatican Council, that the church is the 'universal sacrament of salvation'. Each of these three words is important. The whole church is totally in the business of helping to recognise and promote the action of God's saving grace in every man, woman and child.

Boundaries to God's saving grace?
In this context, I welcomed the searchings of a priest who died a few years ago. His name was Fr Jacques Dupuis SJ. He was European by birth, and he had

worked for several years in cultural and religious set-
tings far removed from European Christendom and
post-Christendom. These were followed by some
years teaching in Rome. He raised sensitive questions
about the saving grace of God at work in other religions. He held the mirror up to the great diversity in
these religions. He became convinced that the church
doesn't monopolise God's saving action in the universe. He was also convinced that belief in Jesus
Christ as the only Saviour leaves space for other saving figures, in various known and unknown ways
related to and drawing energy from the one Saviour.
The reign of God, he insisted, is promoted not by
Christians only but by all men and women of good
will. He saw the urgent need for more collaboration
and dialogue. He was very sure that it is the Spirit of
the saving God who calls us to dialogue.

In all of this, Fr Dupuis caused some concern in the
Congregation for the Doctrine of the Faith. The
Congregation were anxious to counteract any sugges-
tion that any grace comes to us in a way that seems to
bypass and be independent of the universal saving
grace of Jesus Christ. I am confident that, in the spirit
of dialogue advocated by Fr Dupuis, we will find
more and more ways of reconciling our belief in Jesus
Christ as the only Saviour of all with the saving con-
tributions not of Christians only but of all men and
women of good will. We have already found ways of
seeing Jesus as our only mediator and recognising
ways in which he makes all of us agents and carriers
of his mediation.

Dare we hope?

In a similar context I like re-reading Cardinal Hans Urs von Balthasar's book *Dare we hope that all will be saved?* Balthasar never taught that all will be saved. He did teach that we can dare to hope that all will be saved. He dared to hope, somewhat in the way we dare to say 'Our Father', in every Mass. He left all judgement to God who alone is judge of all the living and all the dead. I feel he would have been very happy with Pope Benedict XVI's statement in his first encyclical that God's burning love for his people is so great that it turns God against himself, his love against his justice (par 10).

The ravages of secularism

With the disappearance of many public and recognisable reminders of religion, it isn't always easy to draw the line between believers and unbelievers, between practising believers and non-practising believers. The situation is further complicated by those who say they are spiritual but not religious. We need new and creative ways of calling people to belief, to conversion, to renewal. It is important to remember that 'secular' is itself a good and wholesome word and that it shouldn't encourage a spirit of lamentation. But we are right to be concerned about any secularism that leads to forgetting or dimming the Christian good news.

Concern along these lines has been a constant feature of much of the recent preaching and praying at the shrine of the Lamb of God at Knock. A preacher at a novena early in the new millennium captured many of the feelings of his listeners. The society we call western, he said, is now barely Christian. He described Irish society as de-Christianising fast. He called for a great renewal in the way we celebrate and live out the mystery of the Eucharist. He hoped for a eucharistic revolution which has as its goal the salvation of each single, irreplaceable human being.

It is in the setting of concerns and hopes like these that we have been hearing the good tidings of a new school of evangelisation at Knock. This is a response to the desire of a number of wide-awake lay Catholics to help the young to acquire a really good understanding of their faith. The school is setting out to spread the good news of Jesus Christ, by word, example and lifestyle. The founders of the school are well aware of the reminder of Pope Paul VI that people listen more willingly to witnesses than to teachers (*Evangelisation*, par 41). They are also aware that this can be a word of encouragement to the countless parents whose sons and daughters are following a lifestyle very different from what was taken as the norm a generation or two ago.

No limits
As we help to bring the multitudes to the Lamb, we may well have to face the prospect of smaller numbers of practising Catholic Christians. But this is not to settle for being a kind of religious elite. Leaven is for the whole bunch. The saving work of Jesus Christ knows no limits; it is for the many, for all. The saving

work of all his convinced followers and agents cannot set itself any bounds. When we do set bounds to God's will to save people, we experience the fear that is not from God. We are agents of the plan of an infinitely loving God. The final working out of that plan remains God's secret.

In one of his clarion calls to young people, Pope John Paul II quoted St Catherine of Siena: 'If you become what you are called to be,' she said, 'you will change the world.' Here is a programme not for young people only but for all who believe in Jesus Christ as the one Saviour of all.

Reflection Eight

The Lamb will conquer (Rev 17:14)

In the Christian tradition, our journey through life has often been described in battle imagery:

- This imagery is well highlighted in the Letter to the Ephesians, with its call
    - to take on the whole armour of God,
    - to fasten the belt of truth.
    - to put on the breastplate of faith,
    - the helmet of salvation,
    - the sword of the Spirit. (Eph 6:10-17)

- The last farewell of St Paul is the humble boast of a man who had well used all the armoury of God in life's battles (2 Tim 4:7);

- The battle imagery came to have a prominent place in the hymns of the church.

- Since our childhood days, many of us have joined in the singing of the *O Salutaris* with its 'our foes press on from every side; thine aid supply; thy strength bestow'.

- Every year, the hymn 'The royal banners forward go' was sung in many a religious community and in some public churches. It set the tone for Passion Time and Holy Week.

- For Easter, we had 'Battle is over, hell's armies flee'. We knew, of course, that, in a sense, the battle was only beginning.

The battle imagery was powerfully captured in the Irish eighth century *Lúireach, Lorica*, 'Breastplate' of St Patrick. Some of the sanitised translations of the *Lúireach* miss out on its original sharpness. They have lost the rugged imagery which recognised the poisonous arrows that can come mostly
- from hostile people,
- from dangerous surroundings,
- from treacherous animals,
- from unpredictable weather.

- Many Irish people have been nurtured in the spirituality of the Legion of Mary. The handbook of the Legion draws liberally on the language of the Roman army. Each Legion meeting ends with a prayer that, when the battle of life is over, our Legion may re-assemble without the loss of anyone.

- Many missionary groups, of women and men, have a similar battle imagery embedded in their prayers and devotions.

- It was the same battle imagery that brought seminarians through hard times and made many religious communities accept, without serious questioning, what was a severe and spartan way of life.

- When young men and women took their final vows, it was the practice, in many communities, to give them the gift of a rather stark cross which was very realistic about the wounds of Christ.

Life as a voyage

The approach to life in terms of warfare has little appeal for many young people today. If they had a choice between warfare imagery and voyage imagery, I think most of them would opt for the apparently more benign imagery of the voyage. This occurred to me recently as I re-read the great text that may well come from the same century that produced the *Lúireach* of Patrick; it is *The Brendan Voyage*;

- I became more and more convinced that it is not a record of a Columbus before his time;

- The author may, of course, have drawn on some accounts of historical voyages;

- But those who set out to recognise in it the coast of Norway or Florida or Newfoundland are, I think, reading it with the wrong spectacles;

- We are dealing primarily, I am convinced, with an allegorical composition. *The Brendan Voyage* was an anticipation of some aspects of John Bunyan's *Pilgrim's Progress* with its very colourful descriptions of the mood changes of 'Christian' as he flees from the 'City of Destruction';

- *The Brendan Voyage* was a call to visit the 'Land of Promise of the Saints', to discover the 'Island of Delights';

- From the very beginning, the experience was not all delight. It was very far from today's popular voyages on the Shannon. Indeed it was also very

far from the well-appointed boats that bring pilgrims up the river to the ruins of Clonmacnoise;

- Before Brendan set out in his currach, on unchar-
tered waters, in a sea that was sometimes turbulent
and dangerous, we are told that he was engaged in
nothing less than spiritual warfare;

- In the course of this warfare, he was visited by
Abbot Barinthus;

- At first, the visit of the Abbot generated an atmosphere of sadness. This led Brendan to ask 'Father,
why does your visit make us sad when you have
come to console us? Rather you should give joy to
your brothers. Proclaim the word of God to us and
refresh us';

- It was as a result of the encouraging words spoken
by the Abbot that Brendan decided to go on the
great voyage;

- To accompany him he invited fourteen of his fellow
'warriors';

- Before preparing the currach he started with a
forty-day fast. He made sure to return every year
to fixed locations that were determined by the
liturgical calendar.

The folk memory of many ancient peoples knew of
the good sides and bad sides of voyages. It knew only
too well of the bitterness of shipwrecks and drownings.

- In their closeness to the sea, many of them knew

that the world of warfare and the world of voyage are not that far apart.

- They knew only too well of the bitterness of ship-wrecks and drownings.

- Having to move 'between Scylla and Charybdis' was not limited to any generation of people.

- In his seventeenth century poem about the voyage of those who left England to avoid the Puritan per-secution, Andrew Marvell praised the God who 'the huge sea monsters wracks that lift the deep upon their backs'.

- The fate of the *Titanic*, close to three centuries later, tells us both of continuing human achievement and permanent human limitations.

It would appear that the whole church today needs both the warfare imagery and the voyage imagery.

- At the same time we belong to a winter church and a spring church, a tired church and a church that is rising from its slumbers.

- Many of those in church leadership have 'snow on their roofs', and they are reaching or have reached the biblical quota for the human span on earth (cf Ps 90:10); they feel drained of energy.

- There is a continual temptation to give up the strug-gle, to be demoralised and to experience the kind of sadness that Brendan had before his voyage.

- But some of the best of our contemporary prophets

hasten to tell us that being depressed and being demoralised are not Christian virtues. They remind us that the reign of God is God's dream for the world which he continues to love and that he hasn't stopped dreaming. God is inviting all of us to dream new dreams, to see new visions, and to insert them all into God's own dream.

All of us, young and old, are being invited to embark on a new voyage on fresh waters. This is not just a call to phantasising, even when we have to battle with unsuspected monsters of the deep. The truth is that, for many of us, there are whole treasures in the church's rich tradition, and in the human experience generally, that remain untapped. Maybe this is part of what Pope John Paul II had in mind when he invited us to find a whole set of treasures in what he called the mysteries of light.

Encouraged by the cross of the Lamb

Our battles and our sea adventures will be successful to the extent that we keep immersing ourselves into the whole mystery of the Lamb who, with all his apparent failures, has already conquered and will conquer. The victory of Jesus the Lamb is full of paradoxes, full of apparent contradictions, but it is the victory that will last.

Jesus died the kind of death reserved for terrorists and runaway slaves.

- Even when he had risen from the dead, his cross was seen as a great scandal.

- In the catacombs, the figure of the young shepherd with the sheep on his shoulder was the favoured image to represent the victorious Christ.

- The first representation of the cross didn't come for a few centuries. It is still preserved in Rome. The figure on the cross is a donkey. It would appear that a Roman soldier told his companions that he had become a Christian. They were highly amused and scornful when he told them that the founder of his religion died on a cross. The cross they made is the fruit of their jeering.

- Later Christians did have the courage to make crosses.

- For a while, they refrained from putting a figure on them.

- Over the centuries, we have had crosses from which the victorious Christ has ascended; this is the kind of cross that the fifteen people saw in Knock in 1879.

- Other crosses carry the figure of the victorious Christ.

- Others again, with various degrees of realism, carry the figure of the suffering Christ.

- Each of these ways of depicting Christ's cross somehow brings out the paradox of the power of God being manifested in human weakness.

This saving power of God is what St Paul wished for

when he prayed that he would glory only in the cross of Our Lord Jesus Christ. In the great eighth chapter of the Letter to the Romans, he asked

'Who will separate us from the love of Christ? Will hardship or dangers or persecution, or famine, or nakedness or peril or the sword? ...'

He then went on to express the great paradox of love being generated by what seem to be its opposites:

'... I am convinced that neither death nor life ... nor anything else in all creation, will be able to separate us from the love of God in Christ Jesus our Lord' (Rom 8:35-39).

Here we have the same paradox for which Jesus Christ had prepared his disciples when, having provided them with the wonderful vision of the Beatitudes, declared that they would be hated, reviled and persecuted in his name (Lk 6:22).

This is, of course, no call to either fatalism or complacency. If we are to generate hate, we must make sure that it is for living the gospel and not failing to live it.

- In the spirit of the paradox of what constitutes gospel triumph, we have an annual feast day of the triumph of the cross;

- In Passion time, we welcome the cross as our only hope;

- Even those who reject the cross see some sparks of success in what it stands for; the poet A. C. Swinburne said, begrudgingly: 'Thou has conquered, O pale Galilean: the world has grown grey from thy breath.'

The triumph of the cross
The triumph of the cross of Christ is what, in the words of the title of one of Canon Patrick Sheahan's novels, is called the triumph of failure.

- The triumphant cross has always its shadow side.

- It is true that the fourth gospel presents a great vision of the passion and crucifixion as the lifting up of Christ in glory, and drawing the whole of the human family to himself (Jn 12:32). St John gives us an inspired interpretation of what, in their physical reality, were a succession of shocking and painful events.

- We are nearer this reality of shock and pain in the gospel according to St Mark. In Mark's description of the agony in the garden, the suffering Christ showed symptoms that have been compared to those of a man on the verge of a nervous break-down. Indeed Mark's gospel has been described as a gospel of failure. In its original form it ended on a note not of joy but of terror:
'They went out and fled from the tomb, for terror and amazement had seized them, and they said nothing to anybody, for they were afraid' (16: 8).

And still, it is Mark who begins and ends his gospel on the clear note of good news. Even in its original ending, there is no doubt about the reality of Christ's resurrection. For Mark, this reality must not take away from the reality of the cross that is to be lived by all who wish to enter the glory of the resurrection.

All triumphs are partial
The dark side of the victorious cross of Christ throws light on the fact that all the church's victories are only partial victories.

- The Emperor Constantine gave Christianity a privileged status. We are realising today that his decision left us with a lot of baggage that is alien to the simplicity of the gospel of Christ, in ways that can make us confuse triumph and triumphalism.

- There was a time when we were taught to see the medieval crusades as an unblemished success story. We now see that they also carried the scars of human cruelty, human ambition, human vengeance.

- We thank God for the counter-Reformation and the legacy left us by the Council of Trent. But we see more and more clearly that we belong to a church that is in need of reform, not sometimes but all the time.

- While we are in awe of the stupendous achievements of the Second Vatican Council, there are people in high places who are already speaking of the need for a reform of the reform.

Have we some indelible blackspots?
Recent scandals in the Church have made us cry out with the psalmist:
'If you, O Lord, should mark iniquities, Lord, who could stand?' (Ps 130: 3)

101

- We wonder whether, to draw on some older religious language, we have a dark stain, in the soul and body of the church that, try as we may, we cannot erase.

- In our humiliation, the Lord is showing us what he meant when he said that what is impossible in the eyes of humans is possible with God (Mt 19:25, 26).

- It would appear that God is inviting us now to be re-immersed in the healing wounds of the Lamb who was slain.

- He is inviting us to go to him empty-handed, as St Thérèse, the new doctor of the church, taught us.

- St Vincent de Paul continues to remind us that we will be victorious over any new Goliaths not with worldly armoury but with the smooth stones of gospel virtues (cf 1 Sam 17:40).

- The grain of wheat must keep falling into the ground and dying (cf Jn 12:24).

- We have daily new experiences of the gospel paradox that it is by dying Jesus Christ destroyed our death.

- We are being invited to unite our wounded hearts with the wounded heart of our Saviour.

- He keeps assuring us that he is with us in each of life's battles, in every difficult sailing, in every impossible situation.

Standing on the altar of sacrifice at Knock, under the shadow of the victorious cross, the Lamb assures us of his *Bua*, his victory. He is giving us his encouraging *Beannacht*, his blessing. With a cry of both victory and blessing he keeps saying *'Beir bua agus beannacht'!*

Reflection Nine

Where Mary is at home

The busy parish priest had a rather embarrassing week:

- On Monday, a caller to the sacristy chided him for not encouraging parishioners to join the Lourdes pilgrimage. He had nothing to say in his defence.
- On Tuesday, two pious tourists stopped him to enquire about the special Fatima pilgrimage that was referred to in the Catholic paper. He admitted his complete ignorance.
- On Friday, the leader of the Rosary group worked up courage to ask him why he never had anything to say about Medjugorje. 'And, tell me, what is that?' he asked. The reply came like rapid fire: 'Ah, surely, father, you must know that Our Lady has been appearing there every single day for several years.'
- This time, the busy parish priest threw up his hands, raised his eyes to heaven and said 'I wish that dear woman would stay at home for a while!'

Come to think of it, the dear woman in question is never once, in the scriptures, described as being at home.

- We don't know where she was in Nazareth when the angel of the annunciation came to her (Lk 1:26-38).

- When we next hear of her, she is stepping in haste across the hill country of Judea (vv 39-56).

- We are told that she stayed for three months in the house of Elizabeth; we are not told how her husband Joseph felt about her absence.

- When the time came for her to have her child, she didn't decide for a home birth. She travelled the tedious journey to Bethlehem. Eventually she gave birth in what G. K. Chesterton saw as the place where God was homeless and we are all at home (Lk 2:1-7).

- When the Magi came, they entered the house where the child was with Mary his mother. The location of the house is not named (Mt 2:1-12).

- Neither is the exact time of the gruelling journey into and out of Egypt (vv 13-15).

- Forty days after the birth of Jesus, Mary and Joseph brought him up to Jerusalem (Lk 2:22).

- For each of the first twelve years of his life, they brought him there again for the Passover. It was after one of these celebrations that he was lost and found (vv 41-52).

- Early in his public ministry, he and his mother were together at a marriage feast (Jn 2:1-11).

- On the day when Jesus described what kind of person is his brother and sister and mother, St Mark positions Mary somewhere outside the circle of those who sat around him; even she had to learn to be a disciple (Mk 3:31-35).

- The Christian imagination of later centuries has Mary meeting him on his way to Calvary.

- St John tells us that she stood at the cross of Jesus, in the company of the beloved disciple who was to take her to his house (Jn 19:25-27).

- In the upper room of an unnamed house, she waited, with a large group of disciples, for the coming of the Holy Spirit (Acts 1:14).

A good role model?

It's strange that the woman who is never portrayed as being at home has become the exemplar for all mothers of Christian families. Or is it? Only if we expect the scriptures to provide us with a permanent diary of the Holy Family. What they do give us are glimpses into the mentality of a woman who was somehow at home with a variety of people, in their needs and in their relationships with God and with each other. Helped by these glimpses, the church would later shape her doctrines about and devotion to Mary of Nazareth. It is in her continual and sometimes painful hearing of the word of God and obeying it, and not in the time-conditioned details, that she is presented to all families as a role model.

For many years now, I have been nourished by an approach to Mary to which I was introduced shortly before my Confirmation:

- A visiting preacher spoke tenderly about 'Our Lady of this house'.

- He encouraged us to take home a large prayer card to help us honour Mary under that title.

- The memory of the long-lost card keeps giving me new insights into God's designs for a woman who wishes to be at home wherever people set up house.

- Like the God of Israel in the days that preceded the building of the temple, she keeps seeking a suitable dwelling place (cf 2 Sam 7:5-13).

It is likely that the house in Nazareth where this young Miriam did her mothering comprised one or two rooms that were part of a compound in which a number of families shared the basics for daily living. It has been calculated that on an ordinary day she did about ten hours of the kind of work that included washing, cooking, providing firing, and drawing water. In her continual openness to the needs of the brothers and sisters of Jesus, whoever these were, she could never have developed what has been called the closed-in syndrome. In her final years on our earth, we don't know what life was like for her in the house of John, which has been varyingly imaged as being in Jerusalem or in Ephesus.

Since the time of her unique sharing in the resurrection of her Son, Mary has been housed by the Christian experience and imagination in ways that have differed from generation to generation, from place to place, and from culture to culture.

- She has been imaged in terms of whatever adorns the planet that houses us all.

- She has been dressed and addressed in ways that varied from this house to that house.

- As one specially dwelt in by God, she has been described in tabernacle language and temple language.

With its tradition of courts and palaces, European Christendom tended for long to portray her in 'upstairs' language rather than in 'downstairs' language. The dark, poor, peasant girl tended to become the lady of the royal household, with blue emerging as her most characteristic colour. But this did not keep her from being addressed, in the Litany of Loreto, as the mother most amiable. People found their own ways of giving a local colouring to any descriptions of Mary that seemed distant and remote.

In my home parish, we had a roguish character named Tadhg. When he was an old man, he went to a Lenten station. In the course of the Rosary, he dozed off, but he came to when the priest was calling out 'tower of David ... tower of ivory ... house of gold'. Just then, to the fascination of all, Tadhg came out with a loud 'Blarney castle!' He was ahead of his time when it came to inculturation. It was the same desire to provide the local touch that led the sculptor Albert Power to clothe Mary in a Youghal cloak for a statue in the grounds of All Hallows College, in Dublin.

New lenses

In the years following the Second Vatican Council, the woman who has a special place in 'the household of God, which is the church of the living God' (1 Tim 3:15) has been looked at through a variety of new lenses;

- These include the lenses of liberation theology, of non-European cultures, of gender concerns, of dissatisfaction with various forms of patriarchy. Mary's *Magnificat* has been re-discovered and re-read in perspectives such as these.

- Historical-critical methods have been used to plumb the depths of what is gospel truth about Mary.

- We have been helped to see why and how different generations found new ways of calling her blessed.

- Her perpetual virginity has been presented in terms that, without any denials, emphasise the theological rather than the biological.

- Marian devotions, apparitions, and pilgrimages have been scrutinised from many perspectives.

- Ecumenical dialogue has dealt with such questions as why and how the Catholic language of honouring Mary tended to become inflated at various stages of history.

As Mary continues to be seen through such a variety of new lenses, there has been an ever-recurring preference for 'downstairs' language rather than for 'upstairs' language. The 'upstairs' language is seen to be of value only insofar as it helps us to focus on Mary's influence in high places for those who are in any sense low. The way of our God has always been to reverse and turn upside-down the merely human understanding of 'up'-words and 'down'-words. Mary was indeed the lowly girl whose one desire it was to be at the service of her Lord. It is the very same Lord who has raised her up to share in the glory of her uplifted Son, the slain Lamb. She keeps identifying with his desire to draw us all to where they both are.

The founding truth

The many new lenses provide a fresh impetus to our search for what is the founding idea and image about Mary's place in the household of God. Though each of them has its importance and value, the answer cannot be in such secondary words as co-redemptrix, model, mediatrix.

In the light of its prominence in the Christian experience and tradition, the most satisfactory word remains the mother-word which is also a house-word. All the many secondary words help throw light on the special quality of Mary's mothering. In Mary, God has graced motherhood in a unique way.

That is why we call her 'mother of divine grace'.

- By grace we share in the divinity of Christ who housed himself among us by taking flesh in the womb of Mary. In this housing, Mary became uniquely divinised, uniquely sanctified, uniquely holy.

- No wonder we call her Saint Mary, Holy Mary. She was made uniquely holy by the initiative of the Lord who alone is holy and who is the source of all holiness.

- Our relationship with Mary is situated in the great network of holy persons and holy things that we call the communion of saints.

Mary is the mother of our one Teacher who made it clear that becoming as little children is not just one optional way of entering the kingdom of heaven (Mt 18:3)

- Little children, whether they be small or adolescent or adults, need a lot of mothering.

- It makes full sense that when people like St Thérèse and St Catherine Labouré lost their mothers they sought mothering from the woman who is a unique carrier of the mother-qualities of the God from whom all mothering in heaven and on earth takes its name. There are many senses in which Mary is God-bearing.

Two key moments

There were two key moments in the unfolding of the church's understanding of Mary's mothering. The first was when the bishops at the Council of Ephesus (431 AD) announced to a rejoicing crowd of believers that Mary is *theotokos*, God-bearing, God-mothering. This was not a new word. For well over a hundred years, it had been featuring in a prayer that finally took the shape with which we are familiar:

'We fly to your patronage, holy mother of God …'

The second key moment was when Pope Paul VI announced to a special gathering of the church's bishops that he was declaring Mary to be the mother of the church. After some initial surprise, the sense of this way of naming Mary became clear, even obvious. Mary is the mother of the God-man who made himself one body with his church. She is the mother who wishes to be at home wherever a member of that body is housed or houseless.

Throughout the centuries, many believers have spoken superlative words in praise of Mary's mothering. This is the way of grateful children when they praise their mothers. The language of mothering cannot be programmed. Some people are demonstrative about their mothers. Others are more reticent. It is the same with nationalities and cultures. Good ecumenism seeks exact and measured words when it comes to expressing doctrine, but it also realises that the Celtic and Latin imaginations, for example, tend to be exuberant in the praises of Mary. In honouring Mary as mother, the Catholic tendency generally has been to use the language of the whole heart, in liturgy as well as in popular devotion.

The Knock experience
At Knock, Mary keeps introducing us to the Lamb of God. Over my years at the shrine, I have taken part in many novenas and I have joined many people praying. I must admit that, at first, I tended to look for new approaches, new ideas. What I look for now is

the devotion of what the Bible and the French literary and religious tradition, from somewhat different perspectives, call the heart.

- I have learned that there are as many kinds of devotional response as there are various people praying from their hearts.

- I keep thanking the woman whose presence graced the gable wall of this house of the faithful for giving me something of her own tolerance for this variety.

- Here is the tolerance of a mother who knows all of her household by name, with all their vagaries, eccentricities, and contradictions.

- The only time I'm inclined to be intolerant is when the prayers and the atmosphere have a touch of unreality. People sometimes seem to forget that they are talking to a woman who came to stand by our ancestors at a time when they were poorly housed and sorely tried by famine and emigration, a woman who herself experienced being a refugee and who had to cope with the execution of her only Son. I like the story of Patrick Kavanagh who, when he felt that the singing at Knock was too sanctimonious, turned to his neighbour and, with clear voice, invited him to admire the local field of turnips.

Knock – home from home
When the visiting preacher told us at school about 'Our Lady of this house', I had never heard of Knock. As I pray today at the shrine of unfailing mercy, I like

to address Mary as 'Our Lady of this house and of every house'. Mary's great desire is that each of us will house her Son in our heart and that God will reign in every house. She also invites us to help house those for whom there is no place in any inn (cf Lk 2:7).

The little girl who tripped up on the words of the Angelus and said that Mary was 'handmade by the Lord' got it beautifully right. By the creative action of God's hand, Mary became a special promoter of God's kingdom, God's reign, God's dream for us. She wishes each of us to be a carrier of the good news of the kingdom brought by her Son Jesus in what we now call the third mystery of light. It is on account of her very special involvement in the kingdom of God that we continue to call her queen. When we invoke her as 'Queen of Ireland', we are begging her to promote God's reign in our land.

Knock is an ideal setting for replying to Our Lord's invitation to set up house in his word (Jn 8:31; cf 1 Jn 3:15). The whole message of Knock is well summed up in the invitation dwell
  - in the Lord's anointing (1 Jn 2:27);
  - in his light (1 Jn 2:10);
  - in his teaching (2 Jn: 9);
  - in his love (1 Jn 3: 17).

Mary is the quiet home-maker who is never at home so that we might be always at home, on our journey to our final heavenly home.

Reflection Ten

An atmosphere and a place

Half way through the first decade of the new century, one of our daily newspapers carried a banner head-line. It was introducing an article on visitors and tourists in Ireland in the year that had just ended. Over the year, Knock had been the most visited place in the whole country. Though I knew well that not all visitors and tourists could be called pilgrims, I was pleased with the news. It reminded me to keep look-ing for the essence of what I call the Knock experience. It also led me to stumble on some partial answers.

A place of pilgrimage

Seeing life as an eventful and sometimes hazardous journey is not confined to religious thinking. The word 'odyssey' keeps turning up in surprising places. James Joyce gave a distinctively Irish colouring to an ancient theme when he wrote *Ulysses*.

- Christians generally prefer to see life more in terms of religious pilgrimage than in the language of odyssey, though this, too, can have its religious overtones.

- The Letter to the Hebrews puts it very clearly: 'Here we have no lasting city but we are looking for the city that is to come' (13:14). This, of course, doesn't dispense us from using all our energies to help build up a society of love, justice and peace.

- Even in this daily work of building up, we ask Our Lady of Knock to help us to keep remembering 'that we are all pilgrims on the way to heaven'.

- As followers of Jesus Christ, we have a great tradition of pilgrimage. From quite early in Christian times, believers began to visit holy places associated with the life, death, resurrection and ascension of Jesus. In medieval times, the practice grew considerably and it continues to have a special attraction.

- Our pilgrimages are not exclusive to the land touched by the feet of Jesus Christ. The distinctive Christian pilgrim shells can be found in many parts of Europe. In Ireland, the desire of believers to be 'pilgrims for Christ' was often the beginning of life-long missionary labours throughout Continental Europe.

All Christian pilgrimages tend to have these aspects in common:

- Pilgrims travel light, with a minimum of baggage.

- They are willing to put up with hardship in a spirit of patience and good humour.

- They are willing to carry each other's burdens (cf Gal 6:2).

- They turn strangers into friends.

- They aren't too bothered by the moods of the weather.

- They learn patience in frustrations and they are not very sorry for themselves in these frustrations.

- In a word, they learn many gospel values.

From the beginning, Knock captured and expressed much of this spirit of the older Christian pilgrimages.

- One still hears of the hardships people endured in their long walks to pray at Knock's gable wall.

- Even with the coming of a spectacular airport and vastly improved roads, the walks, the praying and the hardships continue.

- When pilgrims experience rainy weather – an experience that is anything but rare – they recall cheerfully that the apparition took place on a dreary, wet evening.

- In giving their kindly service, the stewards and handmaids capture the spirit of Judy Coyne who herself experienced many setbacks and misunderstandings in her journey of following the Lamb.

- Much of the pilgrim spirit of Knock is expressed in its night vigils. In this watching and praying, pilgrims remind us that we haven't reached home yet and that we await the call of the Master of the house.

A place of silence

In the Knock apparition, no words were spoken. In that silence, the visitors from heaven were saying nothing and saying everything.

- They were alerting believers to all they had said before.

- To a people experiencing hard times, they were saying 'we are with you'.

- In the continuing silence, they were inviting people to do what so many of us are not good at: to listen.

- The invitation remains open; the Lamb of God continues to tell us that, even with all the dross that is surfacing in the church today, he is taking away our sins, having mercy on us and giving us his peace.

- The mother of God is surely saying 'Do whatever he tells you' (Jn 2:5), thereby alerting us to the same call of the Father when he said 'This is my Son, the Beloved' (Mt 3:17).

- With open book, John is inviting us to make our home in the Lord's word (cf Jn 15:9).

- With bowed head, Joseph is telling us that he is continually ready to take the child and his mother (cf Mt 2:13) to destinations not of his choice.

- The angels of God are ascending and descending (cf Jn 1:51), reminding us that earth daily touches heaven and heaven daily touches earth. In Ray Carroll's tapestry in the basilica, the angels seem to be dancing a dance of joy. One is reminded of the invocation in the Litany of the Holy Name: 'Jesus, joy of angels, have mercy on us.'

- The shrine at Knock continues to be a place of the silence of God. In the ongoing shock of the tsunami, in every earthquake, in every human disaster, every time we ask 'where is God in all this?', our silent God invites us to look at and listen to his Son who saved the world at the very moment that he was most helpless.

- The silence of the original figures in the apparition and the continuing silence of God generate an on-going spirit of prayerful silence.

- The shrine is the real power house of Knock. It is at its best when it is most silent. At every hour of the day, every day, people are pouring out their souls there in total silence. Many of them are dealing with a grief too big for words. Many are yearning for healing of body, of mind, of spirit, of relation-ships, of memories. Many will remember the late Mgr Dominick Grealy not so much by the elegant buildings that were his brainchild as by his silent eucharistic praying before the altar of the Lamb, in the twilight hours of many a day.

- The silence of the shrine also pervades the quiet rosaries that groups of people pray as they walk in the shrine precincts. They capture the spirit of the privileged fifteen who, each in their own way, felt the urge to pray, on the great evening in 1879.

A eucharistic place

Three of the church's sacraments are continually celebrated at Knock with a special faith. They are the Eucharist, Reconciliation and the Anointing of the Sick. Each day at the shrine is a call to enter into these divine mysteries with deeper faith and devotion, and to let the glory of the risen Christ shine. In this way, the good news is heard, seen and tasted.

The Knock apparition was an apparition of the Eucharist, in the setting of the communion of saints. Many of the world's Marian shrines have eucharistic overtones. At the Rue de Bac, for example, Mary invited St Catherine Labouré to 'come to the foot of the altar'. But the shrine at Knock is the only one that is directly eucharistic. Every Eucharist celebrates the fact that we are a people reconciled, a people anointed. Of this, Knock is a glowing reminder.

Since 1879, the two most distinguished visitors to Knock were Blessed Teresa of Calcutta and Pope John Paul II. Both were very eucharistic people.

- Mother Teresa continually told her young novices that the body of Christ which they received at Mass, the body they adored during the eucharistic hour, and the body of which the man being taken out of the sewer was a member were one and the same body. Hence her 'five finger exercise': You-did-it-to-me.

- Pope John Paul spoke and wrote much about the human body. His own body became, more and more, a eucharistic body. Indeed he was called, in a dramatic way, to carry the marks of Jesus Christ branded on his body (cf Gal 6:17). He died in the middle of the eucharistic year that he had introduced with a letter teaching that the church draws her life from the Eucharist.

- Knock is true to its call to the extent to which it makes us eucharistic, giving thanks, always and everywhere.

- It is true to its call to the extent that it helps us to be holy, in the company of the whole of the communion of saints.

- To paraphrase the prayer that we have often heard at Benediction, Knock keeps reminding us that we have a 'wonderful sacrament'. It keeps reminding us that God has given us a daily memorial of the victorious Passion of Jesus; it keeps reminding us to reverence the sacred mysteries of his body and blood; it keeps inviting us to keep experiencing in our lives the effects of his redemption.

A place of reconciliation

Knock is a place of good news. Every day it tells us that the Lamb who came to take away the sin of a rejecting world (Jn 1:10, 11) is continually taking away our individual sins.

- The Lamb of God puts our sins in perspective. In his promise of Pentecost, Jesus said that the Paraclete, the Holy Spirit, would prove the world wrong about sin (Jn 16:8). He keeps on sending us this same Spirit.

- He keeps telling us to 'repent, and believe the good news' (Mk 1:15).

- He keeps calling us to a conversion of heart.

- As he gives us 'a new heart and a new spirit' (Ezek 36:26), he keeps taking away our sins.

Is it any wonder that Knock specialises in the sacrament of Penance, of Reconciliation? In the large and spacious reconciliation centre, there are continual opportunities for receiving the sacrament, the whole year round. Prominent in the centre is a large representation of the crucified Christ, with Mary and the beloved disciple at the foot of the cross.

As minister of Reconciliation, a penance I regularly give is 'would you spend a little time talking from your heart to the Lord, to his mother, to the beloved disciple?'

Reconciliation is God's gift of helping the sinner to talk from the heart. When we are reconciled, we talk to the Father from the heart. We talk to his Son Jesus from the heart. We talk to the Holy Spirit from the heart. We talk to the saints from the heart. Estranged husbands and wives are enabled to talk to each other from their hearts. People who up to now have refused to communicate with each other learn to talk to each other, from their hearts. Families find time to talk to each other from their hearts.

In recent years, the church has given us an impressive new *Rite of Penance*. So far, the Rite has had varying levels of success. It will achieve its purpose to the extent that it will help people to be on full talking terms with each other, with the saints, with God.

A place of anointing

To facilitate reflection and discussion, I sometimes used to ask groups of Catholics how many of them had been anointed. Quite often there was a longish silence. Then there came a voice, usually of an elderly person: 'I was anointed last year as I was having a major operation.' This was backed up by a few supportive voices. I then said, 'I thought you were all anointed!' At this, the meaning of the question began to dawn on the group:

- All Christians are followers of Jesus, the Christ who was anointed by the Holy Spirit (Lk 4:18).

- At Baptism, we were anointed twice, with the oil of catechumens and the oil of chrism.

- At Confirmation, we were anointed again with chrism.

- Priests are anointed at Ordination.

- In time of serious sickness, we are anointed in the key areas of forehead and hands.

The oil of the church's sacraments has a purpose similar to that of oil in ordinary usage: to energise, to soothe, to heal, to beautify. In my lifetime, there has been an enormous change of attitude to the sacrament that we used to call Extreme Unction and we now call the Anointing of the Sick. In my early years as a priest, you had to break the news to a sick person that the time may have come for anointing. The order of the sacraments for a seriously sick person was Penance, Eucharist and Anointing. The Anointing was indeed the last sacrament. Nowadays the order is Penance, Anointing, eucharistic Viaticum.

In Ireland, the change in attitude towards the sacrament of Anointing of the Sick has come about largely through the influence of Knock shrine. All through late spring, summer and early autumn, thousands of pilgrims come or are brought, joyfully, to be anointed. The sacrament of Anointing of the Sick has become good news. A result, in the places influenced by Knock, is that priests, instead of having to 'break the news', ask people 'Would you like to be anointed, the way they do it in Knock?'

A popular song speaks of 'pouring oil on troubled waters'. At Knock, we are reminded that, as a people anointed several times over, we are all called to keep pouring oil on the troubles of many people who, to use the imagery of the psalmist, are up to their necks in water (Ps 69:1).

A place of sacramentals
Sacramentals, like the sacraments, are signs of what the church is all about. They help us prepare for the sacraments and they help us live the ideal celebrated in the sacraments. They help us keep interceding, in tune with the whole church. Many of the sacramen-

tals involve the devout use of things we bring for blessing. These include pictures, statues, medals, candles, oil, water. As we enter into the spirit of the sacramentals, we touch, we taste, we kiss, we wear, we sprinkle, we recite a prayer, sometimes an indulgenced prayer. We use all our senses as part of our praise of God, in body as well as in mind and spirit.

Knock is a place of many sacramentals. There are countless statues and images which help keep alive in us the original Knock experience. People reverently touch the stones from the gable of the apparition. After Mass, all over the grounds people ask, 'Would you bless this, father?' They want to bring away from Knock an aid for prayerful remembering. Not all the items are of high artistic quality. But one learns not to judge too quickly; there are many ways in which the human heart can be lifted up to God.

A place of 'miracles' and 'visions'
When you go home after a visit to Knock, your neighbour may ask you, perhaps with some mischief, 'Any miracles, any visions?' Over my years in Knock, I have experienced countless 'miracles'. They wouldn't qualify for the rigorous demands of the Congregation for the Causes of Saints. They are miracles in the literal sense of what causes wonder and amazement. They are the miracles of the opening of people's eyes to what the Book of Revelation calls the 'great and amazing deeds of the Lord God the almighty' (Rev 15: 3). I have met many people who, after a number of visits to Knock, have come to recognise the hand and

love of God in what they had been seeing as misery and even as a curse. I see this as the miraculous touch of God's hand in action.

In the same spirit, I meet many people who have got a new vision, a new way of seeing, at Knock. Their eyes have been opened and they have become 'seers', people who see. What they had seen as unanswered prayer they now see as a blessing, as part of the purification that is an integral part of Christian living.

The prophet Joel foresaw the day when 'Your sons and daughters shall prophesy, your old men shall dream dreams, and your young men shall see visions' (2:28). There is a good youth ministry at Knock but, so far, celebrations at the basilica haven't been highly successful in capturing the imagination of those in their impressionable years. I pray that those of us who are growing old will learn to dream the dreams that will help young people see visions.

A sense of place
Place is important for all of us. A poet put it well: 'I remember, I remember the place where I was born'. The place where he was born was no palace. It included 'The little window where the sun came peeping in at morn'.

The Irish 'patterns', so-called after the local patron saints, gave people a great sense of place. The holy wells, where many people benefited from the healing power of the local water, linked pagan times with Christian times. On patron days and other days, people did the 'rounds' that combined prayer and ritual movement. They followed the journey of the sun, as generations had done, in the same place, before them. There were sermons in every local stone, every local mountain.

The refurbished Knock museum gives us a good sense of place. It helps us thank God for the loving service of many women and men who have made Knock into a place of beauty. It celebrates the 'quiet homes and first beginning' where the grace of God has always been so active. It points us to the privileged place that is the gable wall. Perhaps its deepest message is that God wants us to become holy and to follow the Lamb in whatever place we are now.

Living in or near Knock doesn't automatically make us holier. One is reminded of the medieval Irish pilgrim who went to Rome and learned:
'Who to Rome goes
Much labour, little profit knows;
For God, on earth though long you've sought him
You'll miss in Rome unless you've brought him.'

The most sacred place on earth is wherever you are today.